HOW TO BECOME A BISHOP
WITHOUT BEING RELIGIOUS

Charles Merrill Smith

HOW TO BECOME A BISHOP
WITHOUT BEING RELIGIOUS

DOUBLEDAY & COMPANY, INC.

GARDEN CITY, NEW YORK

1965

THIS IS FOR BETTY
WHOM I MARRIED FOR IRRELEVANT REASONS*

*See Chapter on "Selecting the Clerical Wife"

CONTENTS

What they don't teach you in seminary.

I

Piety and its uses . . . Notes on pastoral attire . . . The car
in front of the manse . . . Living the Inhibited Life . . . Choosing
Art and Literature suitable for the parsonage . . . The value of
the stained-glass voice.

II

The reasons why you must marry . . . The stylish, sexy and
other types of girls to avoid . . . The advantages of marrying a
girl who wants to marry a minister . . . The tremendous advantage of marrying a girl who has money.

III

Entertain the customers . . . Make them cry . . . Make them
feel religious . . . Notes on noteless preaching . . . A preaching
program which can't miss . . . The danger of being specific.

IV

The theology of church finance . . . The pallid sins of nice
people . . . The peace which passeth understanding . . . The
status church . . . Picking the right Negro . . . How to handle
committees . . . The men to cultivate . . . Tell them they are in
charge.

V

How to produce the right feeling . . . The good and the bad

INTRODUCTION

(WHICH JUSTIFIES AND SETS THE TONE OF THIS TREATISE)

Surveys show that American young people put the profession of the clergy near the bottom of the list of occupations they would like to enter, ranking it in desirability just a cut above undertaking and a small miscellany of other dubious callings.

The fact that this is the case is the cause of considerable research, reflection and concern by those ecclesiastical leaders whose responsibility it is to dig up enough clergymen to fill all the vacant pulpits. Why they should be puzzled is difficult to understand because the explanation is obvious —the prevailing public image of the clergyman is not such as to make our American young people want to be one. This is all to the credit of our American youth and speaks highly of its intelligence, ambition and desire to do something significant in the world.

What is this image which fails to attract the favorable consideration of a young man pondering a career?

It is made up of many negative factors—low pay, insignificant work, the high incidence of effeminate types who do choose it, etc. Probably, though, the one item in the public image of the preacher which causes the profession to be

among the first discarded from the area of serious alternatives is the widely held notion that a clergyman has to be
religious. If he is a faithful churchgoer, our young man
probably has come in contact with one or more of the stars
of the church—a Harry Emerson Fosdick, or George Butt-
rick, or Bishops Oxnam, Raines, Kennedy or Pike—and
observed that these are men possessed of bona fide spirituality. He then concludes that it is the spiritual quality of
these men which has brought them to eminence in the
church. Knowing that he is not a genuinely religious person,
the young man crosses the clergy off his list of possible
choices.

Any logician will be quick to spot the young man's error.
He has set up in his mind, quite unconsciously no doubt, a
syllogism something like this:

> Bishop so-and-so is a successful clergyman
> The bishop is a genuinely religious man
> Therefore, one must be genuinely religious to succeed in
> the church.

This logical error is referred to as "the affirmation of the
consequent," and means that one factor has been isolated
and is conceived to have been the cause of the phenomenon
under study (in this case success in the church) when any
number of other factors may be responsible.

Actually, these men taken as examples are geniuses,
gifted as few are gifted, and would have been howling
successes in any vocation they might have chosen. They
have risen to eminence for reasons having nothing at all to
do with spirituality. They would have become bishops (or
achieved equivalent distinction in denominations which do
not have bishops) had they been blackguards and villains
combining the character of a Rasputin with the conscience
of a Richelieu.

In fact, it can be demonstrated with astonishing ease that
the one thing the church cannot abide is a genuinely religious man, and that it takes a generous endowment of other

qualities to offset this handicap if a man is to become a successful clergyman.

It is the author's conviction that the church would attract to it enough candidates for its ministry if only the true nature of the profession were understood and its advantages as a career fully grasped.

So the pay is low—but it is getting better all the time as the gap between supply and demand widens. So the hours are long—but the work, for the most part, is interesting and varied. One begins as one's own boss, an item not included in many other jobs. Hence this book on how to get ahead in the ministry. We will assume that our reader is a young man who has chosen the ministry of one of the standard-brand[1] churches as his life work and is ambitious to get on as rapidly as possible. (We hope, too, for personal financial reasons, that thousands of laymen will want to avail themselves of the rare insights into a fascinating profession contained herein.)

We will assume further that the young man is about to take on the pastoral responsibilities of his first church. If he will read this book, digest it thoroughly and keep it always at hand for quick reference in emergencies, the probability that he will succeed in the ministry is very high indeed.

What they don't teach you in seminary

Some naïve laymen may ask, "But don't they teach these things in seminary?" The answer is that they certainly do not. Seminaries are forced to maintain the fiction that scholarship and spiritual qualities are the only significant factors contributing to a successful ministry. So they spend three years dousing the future clergy with Bible, theology, church history and even Greek and Hebrew, all of which have prac-

[1.] By "standard-brand" we mean Presbyterian, Methodist, Congregational and the like—churches which serve the chunk of the population generally referred to as middle-class. The Episcopal church which identifies with the upper classes, and the sects which appeal to the blue-collar classes are special cases and require specialized treatment which the author is not qualified to handle.

tically nothing to do with success in the ministry and, unless
the new graduate has the good sense to forget it, may prove
a heavy handicap upon his career.

About the only practical teaching in a seminary consists
of lessons (usually bad) on how to write sermons, and
maybe how to baptize babies. The seminaries would be
better advised to devote courses in practical theology to such
subjects as "The Efficient Operation of Duplicating Ma-
chines" and "The Financial Structure of the Sunday School."
These, at least, the new minister could use in his parish
work.

This book will be of vastly more value to a young preacher
than an entire seminary course, and will be an inexhaustible
source of counsel and inspiration in the days and years
ahead. It fills a long-felt gap in theological education, and
will make the transition from the artificial and unworldly
environment of the seminary to the hard, cold world of the
parish ministry, heretofore so difficult and painful, as smooth
and easy as Senator Dirksen's speeches.

The author is a Methodist clergyman who achieved success at a relatively early age (the Methodist church does
not consider a minister ready for larger responsibilities until
he has begun to think about retirement).

He began in a small country church and worked his way
up. So this book belongs not to the genre of "how you ought
to do it" books (usually written by those who have never
tried to do it, or tried and failed), but to that glorious, if
small, class of works authored by those who actually have
done it. Successful men are often inarticulate, or are too
stingy to share their secrets or recognize that the principles
upon which their success is based are so ridiculously simple
that any dolt can master them and thus could bring about
an overcrowded condition at the top.

Fortunately, the author is not only a gifted writer but a
man of generous and sympathetic disposition anxious that
others may also get a whiff of the odor of success he has
found so sweet.

THE PROFESSIONAL STANCE, OR THE TECHNIQUES

OF BEING UNMISTAKABLY CLERICAL

I

Each of mankind's occupations which has managed to pass itself off as a profession acquires through the years a distinctive flavor which, though never reduced to specific formula and always semi-mystical in nature, shapes the personalities of its practitioners and is passed on by them like a torch from one generation to the next.

Somewhere there is, I am sure, gathering dust as its pages yellow and neglected by an unappreciative world, a Ph.D. dissertation documenting the truth known to professional men throughout history but never admitted by them that the proper professional demeanor is much more important in acquiring and keeping clients than one's professional skill.

Thus a doctor of medicine may know everything there is to know about the human body, but if he has a weak chin and a diffident manner no one will believe he can cure anything more complex than chickenpox and he will starve to death unless he goes into research.

A banker may combine in himself an extraordinary grasp of economics with a highly developed sense of how to make money with money without taking risks. But if he affects checked suits and a breezy manner, everybody will take him for an unreliable chap at best, and suspect that he is embezzling prodigious sums and has gone undetected only because of his cleverness at faking the books.

The public expects its professional men to act, talk, eat, drink, think, dress and play in a manner which, in sum, reflects their profession. This is what we mean by and shall hereafter be referred to as "the professional stance."

No other calling demands, for success, the constant assumption of the right professional stance as does the ministry. This is, indeed, the first requirement of an acceptable clergyman. Mastery of it has brought mediocrities to bishop's thrones while its neglect has consigned geniuses to perpetual failure. Though the chapters of this book are not necessarily arranged in order of descending importance, and while every subject treated is of incalculable value to the young cleric ambitious of preferment, the problem of the professional stance is put first because if he cannot learn or cannot stomach this part of the course there is no need to read further. Nothing else will make up for his shortcomings in the matter of the professional stance. It is the *sine qua non*, the Alpha and the Omega, the essential ingredient if the goal is to be reached and worthy ambitions realized.

The stance proper to a clergyman is not easy to describe with precision because it is made up of so many ingredients. It is a mixture, the proper proportions of which defy exact analysis.

Piety and its uses

Nevertheless we must try. To put it in its simplest form, people expect their minister to be serious but not solemn; unworldly but possessed of some practical sense; wise but not smart; gentle but not effeminate; poor but not paupers; unctuous but not pompous; neat but not natty; diligent but not ambitious; upright in his own conduct but not censorious of theirs; forthright but tactful; affable but reserved.

Perhaps the best single word to describe the flavor of personality one must strive to achieve is "pious." This implies that the preacher will gather up in himself a host of qualities and characteristics and distill them into an essence which he exudes at all times, and which advertises unmistakably that here is a man of much prayer and meditation and lofty thoughts, a man who has disentangled himself from the secular, soiling concerns which obsess most men—in short, a clergyman.

Now someone is bound to say that this means a preacher, to be a success, must be religious—a contention which this book is written to deny.

Here we must pause to make a distinction between "religious" and "pious."

A genuinely religious man is, as the sociologists would say, inner-directed. He has deep and abiding convictions usually derived from his faith in God and what he believes to be God's will. Thus he is likely to be socially irresponsible, largely uninterested in the kind of impression he makes on people, often involved in unpopular causes. He tends to be a crusader, frequently intolerant of what he conceives to be injustice or evil. Unfortunately he is usually tactless, making enemies unneccessarily and thus becoming an embarrassment to the church.

We can, of course, admire his courage however ill-conceived, and his zeal however misdirected. But we should not take him as a model. He is the fellow who gives rise to the suspicion that the church is socialistic and brings the whole clerical profession into disrepute. If he wants to make speeches, he ought to hire a hall and leave the care of Christian souls to better-balanced men who understand that the true minister comforts and pleases his people.

The pious man, on the other hand, seems more religious to laymen than the religious man because he tries very hard to fit the image that laymen conjure up when they think of "preacher." It is like people who have so long had frozen orange juice for breakfast that were they served a glass from freshly squeezed fruit, it would taste somehow artificial.

Your church members, of course, will not understand this distinction or even comprehend that there is a distinction to be made. For them "religious" and "pious" are synonymous. It is best not to disabuse them, for if you try, you will likely only confuse them. Always remember that they are not theologians and have no interest whatever in finespun theological ideas. It is better so. If they did understand these things, it would only complicate the minister's already difficult task.

Let me repeat: You can expect to be a successful clergyman without being religious. But never forget that you cannot be a success unless you are pious.

Happily for you, the achievement of a pious, preacherly personality is not overwhelmingly difficult. Anybody, in fact, can manage it with proper attention to detail.

At one time or another in your seminary days, and perhaps quite frequently, some famous preacher stopped by to speak in chapel and—among other bits of advice—exhorted you to be yourself in your ministry, no doubt quoting Phillips Brooks to the effect that preaching is mediating the truth through personality (how often you must have heard that quote).

Now this principle is fine for men like Phillips Brooks and other pulpit stars of strong and spectacular personality. But this is very bad counsel for you. The one thing those of us who are average, ordinary mortals cannot be and expect to succeed is ourselves. Try this and you will, in all likelihood, sink beneath the surface of the profession and never be heard from again.

You see, as ourselves we have tastes, prejudices, habits, manners, idiosyncrasies which often are directly opposed to the pious image we must strive to create, and if we permit their expression, they will ruin the image. No one is naturally pious. It has to be learned. But thousands of successful clergymen will testify that not only can it be learned but that its mastery is the key which unlocked the door marked "advancement" for them.

The fundamental principle here, which you must fix firmly in your mind, is this: Every aspect and facet of your life and personality must be made to reflect the pious image. Let me illustrate how you should apply the principle.

Notes on pastoral attire

One of the more obvious and accurate indices of a man's personality is his mode of dress. In earlier ages one could quite accurately fix a man's station in society and even his occupation by his costume. These distinctions tend to become blurred in a democratic and affluent society, but how a man dresses still tells us a great deal about him.

Now you may have a taste for shaggy sport coats, gay ties, livid hosiery and the like. If so, you must ruthlessly suppress it. Such apparel is associated in the minds of the good people you will serve with flamboyance, worldliness and instability. Who would turn for spiritual counsel to a man in a tweed sport coat? And how many of the saintly Christians in your flock would believe that the prayers of a preacher wearing chartreuse socks could possibly carry to the heavens?

What is needed is a mode of dress which at the same time proclaims what we are but not what we are like. People ought at least suspect that we are clergymen when they look at our clothes.

By now you have no doubt leaped to the conclusion that the answer to this problem is clerical garb. Superficially it would seem to fill the bill. It is an unmistakable uniform, immediately identifying you. It has the virtue of a long tradition and the added advantage of economy. You will at some point in your career, either now or later, be tempted to adopt the clerical collar.

But do not yield to this temptation. Whatever its virtues may be, its disadvantages are far greater.

For one, it conjures up in the minds of the people you will serve pictures of strange rites, fluttering candles and smoking incense. You may count on it that most of your congregation will be hostile to the Roman branch of Christendom, and that they believe (quite erroneously) that only Romans and those with Romish leanings wear the clerical.

Also, if you wear clerical garb while riding a train, some traveling salesman will inevitably mistake you for an Episcopalian and invite you to the club car for a drink, thus putting you in the embarrassing position of refusing his hospitality and confusing his image of the Episcopal clergy.

There are a few—a very few—congregations among the standard-brand churches in which the use of clerical garb can be an advantage. These are, generally, wealthy upper-class suburban churches whose members consider that a pastor in clericals lends tone and class to the church; or congregations in deteriorating areas where the garb is mandatory for identification and protection. But you will be serving middle-class folk for most of your ministry and so must devise a clerical costume which marks you for what you are but does not offend middle-class prejudice.

Experience shows us that a black, oxford gray or navy blue suit (in order of preference) of indifferent cut and average quality combined with black shoes and hosiery, white shirt and dark tie (a small design in color is permissible in the tie but plain black is preferable and helps to identify your calling) will serve as a clerical uniform almost as unmistakable as a reversed collar but without its disadvantages.[1]

Church-goods supply houses sell a suit especially designed for clergymen. It is cleverly made so as to look always just a bit out of style (which it is) and inexpensive (which it isn't). You would be well advised to purchase two or three of these, but it isn't necessary. Any low-priced clothing store stocks what you need.

As you advance in your career you will find it advisable

[1.] In some parts of the Midwest this costume has come to be known as the "central Illinois clerical."

to buy clothes of better quality and cut. Indeed, a more sophisticated congregation will not tolerate the shabby look so prized by smaller and rural churches. But you need never change the color scheme.

Young clergymen should remember not to be too shabby, even when serving the first small church. A congregation bitterly resents a run-down-at-the-heels preacher because it reminds them (and advertises to the community) that it is paying him a shockingly inadequate salary. More than one naïve minister has thought thus to shame a church into raising his salary and discovered that the congregation preferred to solve the problem by firing him. These smaller churches (and some not so small) will be penurious with the preacher in any event, but they expect him to connive with them in concealing it even if he has to borrow money to live on.

This garb has the advantage of being suitable for everyday duty as well as for Sunday pulpit wear. Thus, when you buy a new ensemble you use it first only on Sunday and for weddings and funerals. Congregations will tolerate and even appreciate a bit of elegance on these occasions. You then demote your other suits one notch, the recent Sunday suit becoming the best everyday suit, the former best everyday suit the second best, etc. The author once knew a very successful churchman who even went fishing in the double-breasted black suit, white shirt and black tie which had reached the bottom of his sartorial barrel.

The young clergyman should consider well the many advantages of this solution to the problem of dress before launching out on the uncertain seas of fashion, variety and his own taste.

For one thing, it saves—over an average career of forty years—a staggering amount of time.

There is the time saved daily which other men devote to deciding on which suit to wear, then matching to it hosiery, tie, shoes and other accessories. You are freed from all this

because you made this decision once, when you entered
upon your ministry. Since there is absolutely no variety in
your garb, you need never think about it.

Additionally, other men spend more time than even they
imagine shopping for new clothes. You can do this simply by
calling your haberdasher and instructing him to duplicate
your last order. A conservative computation of time thus
saved over an average career indicates that it would be more
than sufficient for the learning of seven languages or the
writing of a two-volume commentary on the Book of Habak-
kuk.

Furthermore, an invariable costume gives your people the
distinct impression that you are an exceedingly spiritual
man, free of male pride, beyond the clutch of the world's
sticky tentacles in which most of mankind is so inextricably
enmeshed. Yet it is so nearly like what every man wears as
to be socially unobtrusive and to suggest that the wearer—
however spiritual he may be—still is in solid contact with
the real world and can be depended upon to keep the
church budget nicely in balance.

There will come a point in your career at which you will
need to adopt an academic gown for pulpit wear. Some
young men make pretensions to the gown very soon after
ordination, usually with unhappy results. The good, simple
people of your earlier parishes will construe a robe as
"formalism." This weakens their confidence in your theology
as well as your administrative policies.

The proper point at which to put on the pulpit robe must
be carefully calculated and no absolute rule can be laid
down for your guidance here. However, in general, when
you accede to the pastorate of a church with a Gothic nave,
the time has come. People who are not offended by Gothic
architecture will not be offended by an academic gown.
Gowns go well with Gothic.

One exception to this rule applies to the preacher with a
doctorate, whether earned or honorary. Any congregation,

no matter how unsophisticated, will be proud of this and want it flaunted. Since it is obviously inappropriate to sew doctor's bars on a sack suit, a gown is clearly indicated.

The car in front of the manse

Another obvious index to a man's personality is his motor-car. Psychological research tells us that we reveal a great deal about our inner selves by our choice of an automobile. It is at the same time a sign of our station in society, a way of expressing our hidden frustrations and subconscious long-ings and, incidentally, a means of transportation.

Now to a pastor a car is absolutely essential. Of necessity he will spend a great many hours in it. It represents the largest single item of expense in his budget after food. The selection of the "right" car, therefore, deserves considerable attention.

Since any make of automobile, when new, will furnish adequate transportation for the clergyman, the selection should be made on the basis of less tangible factors.

The first of these factors we will examine, and by far the most important, is that the automobile he drives is for the preacher a potent instrument for creating the proper pious professional stance. What we need to arrive at is a reliable formula for combining make, model and color so as to obtain the optimum image reflection. This problem is fur-ther complicated by the fact that what is appropriate at one stage of your career would be wrong for another stage.

The beginning clergyman will avoid a great deal of diffi-culty in the years ahead if he will get well in mind the general outline of the automobile market, classify it as to cost, luxury, public image, etc. He will then bracket the available selections in terms of appropriateness in relation to the size, affluence, educational level and sophistication of his congregation. But let us hasten to simplify.

It is well to envision, as a beginning point, the low end of the market, those makes, models and colors which would be suitable for the pastor of three small rural churches whose

members think that Calvin Coolidge was the greatest states-
man of our century. This is represented by one of the
popular economy compacts. Purchased in the least expensive
body style and most conservative color, it says of its owner,
"This is a thrifty, sober man who makes no rash decisions,
whose money is not at the mercy of his emotions, whose true
values are spiritual, who is not seduced by the trifling, the
flashy and the frivolous."

Thus we arrive at a black standard two-door Falcon
sedan as the ideal automobile for the beginning clergyman.
Admittedly our society has liberalized in attitudes toward
the motorcar since Henry Ford manufactured nothing but
black cars. A dark green Chevy II[2] with an automatic trans-
mission would not be too daring for most small congregations. Such a car is always "safe," although a substantial
urban church generally expects its pastor to drive something
a bit larger and less austere.

Now let us envision the upper end of the market. Most
people think of a Cadillac as a symbol of the ultimate in
luxury, price and status. They consider a convertible to be
the final frivolity in body styles, and associate the color red
with flamboyance and daring. A red Cadillac convertible
sums up, therefore, everything you must avoid in the selection of your vehicle, just as the black two-door Falcon
sedan sums up everything that is correct for you in a motor-
car.

You will never consider, then, a Cadillac, a convertible of
any make, nor red in any model.

With these sound principles in mind, you may vary the

---

2. The author is aware that some small foreign cars are cheaper to
buy and maintain than American compacts. One runs the risk with
them of being accused of "inverse car snobbism," however, as well as
laying oneself open to the suspicion that one is less than a 100-per-
cent American. The author is preparing a monograph "Is a Foreign
Automobile Suitable for the Clergyman?" which will appear subse-
quently in *The Preacher's Home Companion* and may be included
in later editions of this book.

make, model and color of your car as you climb the ecclesiastical ladder.

For example: nearly any church which pays a pastoral salary of more than $7000 per year will tolerate a hardtop sedan in the parsonage garage and will not object to one of the more muted colors in metallic paint. A handy chart to aid you in your selection is included on page twelve.

You will note the overlapping of some makes and models. This simply means that the maximum selection suitable for one salary range can also be the minimum selection for the next higher range.

One complicating factor in the car purchase problem is the occasional automobile dealer you will inherit with your congregation. There is no way to avoid buying from him. He knows he has you and will overcharge you by the amount of his annual contribution to the church (which, fortunately for you, is unlikely to be large).

Living the Inhibited Life

Everybody has his own little peculiarities, ways of doing things, characteristic facial expressions, reactions to others, moods, affectations, etc., which we lump under the heading of personal habits and which total up to our public personality.

Most people find it expedient to control and develop these habits along lines which they would not take if people were free of all inhibitions. (This is why a quiet, polite, gentlemanly fellow may become loud, uncouth, insulting and lecherous when drunk, because alcohol ingested in sufficient quantity removes these civilized inhibitions.)

It is absolutely essential to the preacher's image that he hedge in his natural inclinations with a rugged set of custom-made inhibitions. Let us illustrate.

It is essential to the achievement of the pious image to project a mild but distinct quality of asceticism. The average Protestant church in America is made up of people who are only a few decades removed from their Puritan ancestors

	1st Pastorate Salary Range $4000–5500		2d Pastorate Salary Range $5600–7000		Large Urban Parish Salary $7100–10,000
MAKE:	Any compact	OR Chevy, Ford, Plymouth	Dodge, Pontiac, Catalina	OR Mercury, Buick LeSabre	Chrysler 300, Olds 98, Buick Electra
MODEL:	2-door sedan	OR 4-door sedan	4-door sedan or hardtop		4-door sedan or hardtop
COLOR:	Black, dark green, dark blue	OR gray, lt. green	Black, biege	OR Metallic blue or green	Any color but pastels or red

and who have not yet succeeded in shaking themselves free from the conviction that a Christian is one who doesn't enjoy this world very much.

The author is aware that this is a heresy, but the relevant point is that it is a popular heresy. You don't need to preach it, for you know better and you don't want to be blatantly dishonest. But you do need to practice it.

A prudent preacher, therefore, will never use alcohol or tobacco.[3] He will avoid card playing and dancing and the use of profanity. He will never, never tell an off-color story, and when one is told in his presence will react with a slight frown followed by a very brief, tolerant, superior smile which will make the teller feel sinful and embarrassed.

Your people do all of these things, of course, but they feel vaguely guilty about doing them. If you will remember that your congregation, although it does not understand this, pays you to be good for them, it will help you in the formation of your public attitudes. You are, in a very real sense, the modern Protestant equivalent of the ancient Jewish scapegoat upon which the sins of the people were heaped and thus expiated. The esteem in which you are held and the more tangible appreciation in the form of salary and emoluments will be directly proportional to your skill in fulfilling this role.

A preacher who appears to be getting a lot of fun out of life does not impress the laity as a very good scapegoat. He may be popular at Rotary Club, but he will be poorly paid by the people he serves and constantly in danger of losing his pulpit.

Your pleasures, then, should not be of a vigorous nature. It is a pity that croquet is no longer popular for it is the ideal recreation for the clergy. No one gets very excited about it, no one swears over a poor shot, it is inexpensive, and it doesn't work up a sweat.

[3.] Episcopalian and Lutheran clergymen and Presbyterians serving country-club-type congregations are exempt from these restrictions.

Checkers is a wholesome, if boring pastime. Chess is permissible only in a college community where it is not disadvantageous for a preacher to be thought intelligent. Tennis is a sport of good repute, but a little strenuous. Younger clergymen (modestly attired) may play it without undue criticism. Otherwise, things being what they are, the habit of extensive walking is the recreation best suited to the clerical image.

The one sin permitted the preacher by his congregation is the sin of gluttony. Not only will your people permit it, they will urge it upon you at every opportunity, to the accompaniment of coarse humor about how preachers like to eat.

The reason for this, while not apparent to the people, is not hard to discover. Having denied you every other indulgence of the flesh, they ease their unconscious guilt by removing all limits on this one. And since most of them are dieting, it has the added advantage of making them feel spiritually superior to their pastor at one point at least.

It must be pointed out, though, that you are not expected to be fat. How you are to eat prodigously and remain slim is one of the more trying perplexities of your profession, but a fat man can hardly manage to look ascetic. It will be thought that either he is worldly and grossly sensuous, or that he has a clutch of emotional disturbances gnawing away at his psyche, the pains of which he assuages by incessant gourmandizing.

Space does not allow us to detail every item which can contribute to the total image we are seeking to create. The rule to remember, however, is that the little things add up to the big thing.

Choosing Art and Literature suitable for the parsonage

The young clergyman, for example, may be negligent about the reading matter reposing on end tables or carelessly thrust into magazine racks in the parsonage living room.

You will discover that parishioners who drop by the house

(and there will be many of them) nearly always take note of what the preacher is reading and report it through the parish grapevine.

Novels in plain sight must be of the most chaste type. The works of Lloyd Douglas, Frank Slaughter and the religious novels of Thomas Costain are examples of the kind of thing you should have on hand for display purposes (there is no necessity for reading them). *Reader's Digest* condensed books are perfectly safe because everyone knows they have had the racy passages leached out of them.

For magazines you will do well to have always in some obvious place the current issues of *Time* to show that you are a man who keeps up with the world, and *The Saturday Evening Post,* which identifies you with the solid middle-class virtues and suggests that you are politically conservative.

You will naturally always have copies of your denominational publication and other religious journals in abundance lying about. They are, in the words of a celebrated fictional divine, filled with "holy bilge and sacred bunk." But again, you do not need to read them (unless your taste runs to that sort of thing), just display them. They complete the picture, add the right touch and tone, solidify the image.

Judgment must be exercised, too, in the art with which you adorn the parsonage walls.

The salient rule here is that any painting or reproduction displayed must be representational. If your taste runs to Picasso or Paul Klee, hang them only in the privacy of your bedchamber (and take them down on the days your wife entertains the Ladies' Society, because the ladies will expect the use of the master bedroom for a cloakroom, and may mistake any abstract art for examples of arcane erotica).

It is best to stick to reproductions familiar to the least sophisticated members of your congregation. This limits your choices to a relatively few paintings, most of them bad, but you will just have to make the best of it.

Every preacher should possess and display in the most prominent place in his house (over the fireplace mantel, for example) a large and well-framed copy of Warner Sallman's "Head of Christ." That this is a badly done, repulsive piece of art is beside the point. It is the most popular "Christ" among American Protestants, and your possession of it not only puts the proper pious stamp upon you (for Sallman's is a very pious, otherworldly Christ indeed) but it identifies your taste with that of about 99 per cent of your congregation, which is very good for you.

Da Vinci's "Last Supper" is also appropriate. You may feel, as does the author, that this is one of a great painter's dubious efforts, but it is religious and it is identifiable by anyone who has advanced culturally to the level of reading without moving the lips.

For relief from religious art, a landscape or two (which should be nearly indistinguishable from photographs) and maybe a still life are acceptable. You may even use a still life which includes a bottle of wine so long as the setting is clearly foreign. Even the president of the local chapter of the Women's Christian Temperance Union understands that foreigners are less enlightened about the joys of total abstinence than good solid American Christians and will not think ill of you. And there will be many a night when, exhausted from a day of dealing with cantankerous saints, you will contemplate such a painting with considerable pleasure.

In your early pastorates a small felt banner reading "God Bless Our Home" and perhaps a wooden plaque with the Lord's Prayer burned into it will complete the *objets d'art* necessary to clinch the image. By your third church, though, they should be omitted lest you be considered a bit bucolic.

You need not be told, I am sure, to avoid any art which contains nude figures. American Protestants have discovered sex, of course, but they are slightly ashamed of it and prefer to think that their preachers haven't.

Whatever you do, you must not show much interest in

the arts. Businessmen associate artistic proclivities with un-reliability and the Democratic party and will be certain that any fiscal policies you advance can bring nothing but ruin to the church. Also, the "arty" image is fatal to the pious image. The two are fundamentally incompatible.

The value of the stained-glass voice

This chapter on the professional stance does not pretend to cover every possible life situation through which the image can be expressed, because it would be impossible to do so. The point is that any and all public situations in which you are involved are not only opportunities to reinforce the image with which you seek to invest yourself, but it is mandatory that you use them as such.

Remember that the pious, or professional, stance has to be learned. Clergymen of your acquaintance whom you have always thought of as having been born pious will immediately come to mind. But were you to question them (and assuming that they would give you an honest answer), they would tell you that they, too, had to practice the stance with all the single-minded devotion of a concert pianist or a professional golfer before they achieved their present levels of proficiency. True professionalism in any field demands unremitting practice.

This means that you must take care not to shuck the image completely even in the privacy of the home and family life. One successful and well-known minister claims it is absolutely essential to speak in a "stained-glass voice" even to your wife and children.

There will no doubt be protests among you that the deliberate and calculated effort to achieve the pious image makes a man a phony and will thus do lasting harm to his psyche. It is dishonest, some will say, to pretend to be something you are not.

Let me put your mind at rest on this.

Be reminded, first, that everyone pretends to be a better, more interesting, more important person than he really is.

You are only carrying this "erecting a front" to a sensible, well-planned extreme.

Second, you are doing this for a good cause. Church people expect their preachers to be pious, indeed demand that they be pious. They are disturbed, upset and angry when their pastors do not fit the stereotype of preachers which they have so long held sacred and which symbolize for them the true man of God. To refuse to conform to their blessed prejudice is to diminish your effectiveness as their spiritual counselor and leader.

Third, it is only a short time, relatively, before the assumed image becomes the "true you." Console yourself, during your first year or so of image building with the thought that before long the strain of pretending, the feelings of guilt will pass. Soon you really will be pious. Soon you will feel guilty on those increasingly rare occasions when you momentarily forget to keep the image firmly in place. You will feel guilty, though you may not believe it now, when you are not pious.

Fourth, and of primary pertinence, there is no other way to assure yourself a level of success in the ministry commensurate with or exceeding your natural endowments for doing the Lord's work.

II

The most important one piece of equipment the aspiring clergyman will acquire is a wife. So vital is the wife to the success of the minister that the care he should exercise in selecting her cannot be overstressed.

Other authorities have shown how the wrong kind of wife can hamper and inhibit an otherwise promising executive career. The harm that the worst imaginable executive wife can do to her husband's career, however, is but a negligible annoyance compared to the shattering effect an unsuitable parsonage spouse has on her consort's labors in the Lord's vineyard.

It may be that you are already married. Clergymen, for some reason which needs more research, have an unfortunate tendency to marry quite young. And when a man marries young, he has almost always married for the wrong reasons so far as his future professional success is concerned.

If you find yourself in the difficult position of beginning your ministry equipped with a wife you married because you fancied you were in love, or because you found her charming, or because you were sexually attracted to her, or for any other irrelevant reason, you are up against what

will probably turn out to be the most baffling problem of
your professional life. Barring the unlikely possibility that
by chance and blind luck you picked the right type for the
parsonage (which would be the equivalent of breaking the
bank at Monte Carlo or filling an inside straight) about all
you can do now is to institute a program of education designed to bring her up to minimum standards of performance (which you should begin by calling her attention
to this chapter).

However, you should be cautioned against excessive
optimism as to the probable results. Observation of such
educational efforts have been depressing, the woman who
marries a minister without understanding the nature of the
demands his profession places on her usually proving quite
intractible when it is suggested, even with considerable tact,
that she make over her personality to the satisfaction of her
husband's present and anticipated congregations.

However, we will assume that we have caught you in
time, that you are reading this while still a bachelor and
without any unbreakable alliances entangling you, that you
are legally and morally in a position to select a wife in
accordance with the principles and the wisdom here
offered.

You must begin by fixing in your mind the fact that
your chosen work has already determined the qualities you
will look for in a wife. She must be selected to fit these
specifications.

Now if you have been corrupted by the silly ideals of
romantic love poured over us in a sticky and seemingly inexhaustible cascade by the movies, television and the
popular women's magazines, you may at first recoil from
this suggestion. But upon mature and calm reflection, you
will see how very right is this principle.

You will not deny, surely, that any reasonably healthy
female is capable of performing all the functions of a wife.
She will be able to cook, keep house and bear children.
Further, if romantic illusions are necessary to your emo-

tional well-being, you can check with any psychologist and be assured that these depend not on the loved but on the lover. Or to put it simply, it's all in *your* head. Therefore, it places no exceptional psychological demands upon you to invest any girl with the aura of romance.

It should be clear to you by now that the proper sequence of events is to select a girl who meets the predetermined specifications and then fall in love with her, rather than allow your romantic fancy to light upon just any young female who happens to appeal to you for irrelevant reasons (some of which were mentioned earlier), and then have to make the best of it if she turns out to be—as she almost surely will—poorly fitted for the role she is expected to assume.

The reasons why you must marry

If by now you are contemplating the advantages of clerical celibacy (which would not be an unreasonable reaction considering the problems involved in your selection) dismiss such thoughts at once. Protestant Christians expect their clergy to marry. The folklore of the trade holds that it is necessary for a minister to marry in order to set an example of Christian family life.

You will want to pretend that this is true, just as you will find it expedient to pretend that you dwell in a state of marital bliss the calm waters of which are never rippled by a cross word, let alone a quarrel. The nervous strain involved in such pretensions is of awesome proportions, and is known to have pushed parsonage wives into emotional breakdowns and turned parsonage children into church-hating delinquents. However, all good things in this life are bought at a price.

The real reasons why you should marry are, of course, not at all related to the folklore.

First, a clergyman who remains unmarried for more than a year after graduation from seminary is suspected of being abnormal, immoral or chicken.

Second, there will be those who will speculate that he has taken St. Paul on marriage too seriously and has made a secret vow of celibacy. So far as your parishioners are concerned, you may be as celibate as a Cistercian monk, but they will insist that you practice it within the married state.

Third, somewhat more than half of your congregation will be women, and all women—single, married or widowed (including grass widows)—resent a male eligible for marriage who chooses to remain unwed.

Fourth—and here is the overriding argument in the mind of the congregation—since the church owns a parsonage and already has arrived at a salary figure below which it cannot go and maintain its conviction, however illusory, that it is a humane institution, it is only sensible to get two employees for the price of one. Therefore, it boils down to a business proposition. It would be damaging and vulgar to admit to this, however, so the tradition and the folklore was manufactured to mask it.

Actually it is very good business from the church's point of view. Most girls are piano players of sorts, and anyone can learn to operate a typewriter or mimeograph. Add to these accomplishments the intellectually untaxing duties of Sunday School teaching, choir singing, ladies' aid work and a miscellany of other small parish chores all of which your wife will be expected in your first small churches to perform (it's part of the tradition) and you have a job analysis which, were it filled by a salaried employee, would require no small addition to the annual budget. Hence the tradition of a married clergy.

Let us assume that you are now convinced that you have no choice but to marry—and not because, as St. Paul so delicately put it, your only alternative is to burn. The exhausting life of the parish ministry and cold showers eliminate or greatly minimize this problem. The frightening alternative to marriage for you is the unappetizing prospect of a career in back-country or run-down city parishes.

To be sure Phillips Brooks and a few others made it big in the ministry without taking unto themselves wives. But they were the rarest of exceptions. If you want to be a preacher and a bachelor, be prepared for a dismal future and renounce now the hope for status, prestige, emolument, luxury and all of the spiritual joys which accompany a plush suburban pastorate. The author does not question the preacher's right to take a vow of chastity, but he'd better darn well understand that a vow of poverty goes along with it. However, it is unlikely that anyone who has read this far is uncommitted to the ideal of advancement in his chosen profession. So let us proceed to the rules for selecting the suitable clerical wife.

We are immediately struck by the realization that it is far easier to describe what the suitable wife for the ambitious clergyman is not than to delineate the precise qualities and characteristics which make her suitable.

The stylish, sexy and other types of girls to avoid

Since the one thing the congregation will notice first and most often about her is her appearance, special attention must be paid to this facet of her personality. To cover the rule in a sentence, she must not be beautiful, stylish or sexy.

This does not mean that she should be homely and frumpy. The smallest rural circuit will appreciate a presentable preacher's wife. And when pulpit committees from larger churches come looking you over, they will take a good look at her, too. More than one clerical career has been nipped in the bud when a committee thought they had their man but, finding that taking him meant taking a shabby-looking wife too, decided to look elsewhere.

Nor does this rule prohibit you from marrying a real stunner. Any woman, even if she won the Miss America contest in a walk and brings on attacks of pop-eyes and shortness of breath among the males present when she strolls through a hotel lobby, can learn to tone down these assets to a level acceptable to most congregations. She can go easy on the make-up, wear serviceable but not overly stylish dresses and sensible shoes, and go to a hairdresser of indifferent skill. This will do wonders, in reverse, for her appearance without rendering her in any way unattractive.

If she asks why she must submit to this sort of thing, remind her that the women of the congregation actually run the church, either by getting a stranglehold on the key committees or by telling their husbands how to run it, or both. So a preacher really has to please the women if he expects to keep a pulpit, and give the distinct impression that he knows how to please the women if he expects to get a better one.

There is no possibility of pleasing the ladies if he flaunts a knockout of a wife, for she is a constant threat to their peace of mind, and he will have nothing but trouble. If she is so lovely as to make the ladies of the church feel homely, and so stylish as to make them feel dowdy, his prospects for a shining career in the church, which may be otherwise quite bright, are dimmed by several thousand candlepower. The ladies simply will not put up with such a woman in the parsonage.

And for a clergyman to marry a woman who possesses an abundance of sex appeal is absolutely fatal to his career. The men of the congregation will appreciate her, of course, which is the first reason that their wives won't.

Remember, too, that your image depends in part on the inability of the congregation to imagine you engaging in sexual intercourse. That you have children, and that practically nobody nowadays believes the stork brings babies might be thought to destroy this part of the image. But it is not as serious as you might suppose, although there is something to be said for the childless clergyman (including the economic facts of parsonage life).

But children in the parsonage do not confuse overmuch the image of the preacher as a member of a third sex. If they think about it at all, the congregation will imagine that the accouchements were accomplished through immaculate conception or parthenogenesis or artificial insemination. At the very worst they should be able to believe that their pastor was only fulfilling his social responsibility of fathering children and that he really didn't enjoy the procedure essential to this end very much. It is not easy to believe this, of course, if the pastor's wife has a high-voltage look about her.

From your own point of view, an overly attractive wife can be a millstone around the neck of progress in your profession. She will be a constant distraction to you, and you will be tempted to spend time with her much better invested in getting on with your career.

Such an eminent authority on executive success as Vance Packard has pointed out that in the world of big business the man who is entirely happy with his home life is not a good bet for heavy responsibility. One way to spot a real comer in the corporation is to find the fellow who is a bit discontented with his marriage.

As a pastor you should never even entertain the thought that you are discontented with your marriage. The same end can be achieved by refusing to become too much absorbed in it. A good, plain-looking wife whom you like and about whom you can think with affection but without passion is an inestimable aid in directing your primary devotion to your church and its duties. If it is no hardship to stay away from home, you will not have to fight frequent spiritual battles over the choice between one more pastoral call or that important committee meeting and an evening at home. Any pro will tell you it is that extra effort, that last push which wins the game. So if getting home to the wife is not a prospect which is irresistibly attractive, then no great sacrifice is entailed in absenting yourself in order to get in a few more licks on the job.

It will not occur to the members of your flock that you are working hard and putting in long hours because you would just as soon work as to hang around the house. They

will conclude that you are driven by devotion to your calling and an acute sense of responsibility toward the welfare
of your church. There is no need to rectify their thinking
on this matter, of course, and it is well if you think along
the same lines.

Perhaps the best possible approach to the problem of
clerical mate selection is to imagine that you are planning
to employ an assistant pastor and are scouting the prospects. This will focus your attention on the genuine issues
at stake and compensate for the normal male irrelevancies
which becloud the true values we should seek. Never forget that you are a clergyman first and a man second.

The advantages of marrying a girl
who wants to marry a minister

Another excellent rule to follow as you make your selection
is "look for a girl who is looking for you." By this we mean
that you can hardly go wrong if you choose a young lady
who has set out to marry a preacher.

Be assured that there exists at any given moment a fair
number of nubile females who actually have marriage to a
clergyman as their goal in life. The advantages, for you, of
an alliance with a young lady in this category cannot be
dismissed lightly and should be sufficient to stimulate you
to a diligent search for her.

For one thing, she will be likely to understand what she
is getting into better than a girl who would find a registered
pharmacist as acceptable to her as a clergyman. Further, it
can be asserted that she will really enjoy the role of
minister's wife, and will not find it tedious, boring and
artificial as many girls do. She will accept without com-
plaint the economic restrictions imposed on her by your
profession, and won't swear at the good matrons of the
Women's Society even in private.

Also, psychologists who have done research on the subject report that girls who want to marry preachers generally
have a low sex drive and, convinced by the pious Prostestant

image of the clergy, believe that an ordained husband will be modest in the carnal demands he makes of her. (It is inevitable, of course, that it won't always work out this way for the girl since a few lusty characters do manage to find their way into the ministry, but the odds are very probably in her favor.) You can readily see that if you choose such a girl you will be gaining a dividend of time and energy in amounts nearly beyond calculation which can be applied to your professional duties. It gives you an advantage over your clerical competitors whose marital situation is less fortunate which seems almost unfair.

The tremendous advantage of marrying a girl who has money

The author hesitated long before including the following final word of counsel, knowing that he risks misunderstanding and that to some it will seem indelicate. However, be that as it may, he decided to run these risks because of the joy it may bring to those who heed it. The counsel is this: When choosing a wife, make every effort to locate one who has some money of her own.

It is not so difficult as you might think to bring off. The population has a glut of marriageable females and some of them have already, or will in time, come into an inheritance. Why should not you, too, the Lord's faithful and self-sacrificing servant, share in this bonanza?

You will be gratified, should you carry out this counsel, to discover how even a few hundred extra a year will palliate the hardships, the meager income of your early pastorates. And even in your later and better-salaried days, your wife's remittance will mean the difference between relaxing in comfort in an air-conditioned hotel, and dining in the better restaurants or sweating it out in some flea-bag while you subsist on hamburgers and beans during the frequent conferences and conventions you will be expected to attend. And if you are careful enough or fortunate enough to marry a girl who is really loaded, you will take trips to the Holy Land and vacation in Florida while your ministerial brethren who are forced to live on their own income will curse their grocery bills and envy you.

And if you consider this suggestion to be crass and revolting materialism, keep in mind the fact that your larger income means a larger tithe (10 per cent of income after taxes) which you can devote to the Lord's work. This thought should be sufficient to tranquillize any fears that you are succumbing to the lures of this present world.

If you can manage to marry a bit of money, the esteem in which your congregation will hold you is bound to be quite high. The one thing all Americans respect without qualification is money. And the classic Protestant ethic holds that when a man is blessed with material rewards it is a sign that he has found favor in the eyes of Jehovah. Since you are theologically sophisticated, you may have your doubts about the validity of such an ethic, but your congregation won't.

Marriage is always fraught with uncertainties and incalculables. No one can ever be certain, in advance, that a marriage will work out along the lines planned and hoped for. Everyone should enter it rationally, realistically, and only after the suitability of the intended partner has been scrutinized as carefully as possible. And what everyone should do (but not very many do do, or the divorce rate in our country would be much lower than it is) the clergyman must do if he has expectations of advancement in his profession as well as a felicitous atmosphere in his home.

With the counsel here given, you will be able to reduce the hazards in this extremely hazardous enterprise, and choose a mate who not only will grace your parsonage but be a co-worker in and an ornament to your holy calling.

III

Unless you attended a really first-rate seminary, which is unlikely since there are so few of them, probably you have been taught that a clergyman's first, primary, basic, fundamental, highest, most sacred, most precious function, duty and privilege is to preach.

Chances are you have been dunked in the doctrine that you will ultimately rise or sink in your chosen work on the basis of your performance in the pulpit. Also, if you were so unfortunate as to fall under the spell of a persuasive professor of preaching with liberal inclinations, you may even believe that you should take some long-bearded Old Testament prophet as your ideal and denounce the supposed evils of our society as, for example, Amos whacked and lacerated the society of his day. This would certainly be a bad mistake. After all the only pulpit Amos ever filled was at Bethel—and he was requested to resign after one sermon.

At any rate, the interpretation of the minister's role largely in terms of his preaching function is encouraged by the laity which supposes that the delivery of a weekly homily constitutes the clergy's major work load. You will get awfully sick of the jibe "Pretty good pay you get, Reverend, for working one hour a week." This is delivered always by the coarse, hearty type of parishioner who thinks it is original with him. It is best to smile if you can manage it.

However, if you care to achieve more than very modest success in the church, you must (1) convince yourself that all this business about preaching being your most important task isn't true and (2) convince your congregation that it is.

Let me elaborate. If you believe preaching to be first and most important in the work of a minister, you will naturally devote the largest slice of your time and energy to the preparation of your sermons, thus robbing yourself of the opportunity to address yourself to the genuinely vital and productive duties of your calling.

Any veteran cleric who has gotten anywhere at all will assure you that preaching is quite secondary in his scale of values. Yet we keep getting, year after year, floods of fresh seminary graduates who are enamored of the image of the pulpiteer. They buy an astonishing number of books. They use up the good working hours of the morning for study. They have a tendency to write out their sermons, polishing and repolishing them. And some of them even plan their sermons for the entire year ahead. This is expensive in terms of precious time and your meager supply of ready cash (books are frightfully costly these days). It is also entirely unnecessary.

However, your laymen should be allowed the illusion that preaching is your number one task because the illusion can be made to pay you rich dividends.

Fix firmly in the structure of your basic operating philosophy the fundamental fact about the ministry of the pulpit, which is: "It is ridiculously easy and requires but a negligible chunk of your time to be a popular pulpit personality."

Now if this is true (and rest in the confidence that it is), then it requires no especially gifted imagination to grasp the possibilities here. So long as your congregation is enthusiastic about you as a preacher, the following benefits will accrue to you:

1. The congregation will be inclined to charity concerning your weaknesses, and you are bound to have some. ("Well, we must remember that good pulpit men are hard to come by," they will say—a judgment which usually buries any criticism of your deficiencies.)

2. When your church members don't see you they will assume that you are sequestered in your study poring over the Scriptures, the philosophers, the post-Nicene fathers (they haven't, of course, the remotest notion of what a post-Nicene father is) adding to this intellectual sour mash the catalyst of your own reverent insights and thus distilling the spiritual booze which will give their souls a hearty wallop when you serve it up on Sunday morning. So long as they assume all this, they will not wonder how you spend your time, which permits you a considerable amount of personal freedom.

3. Your reputation as a superior pulpit man will get around, and better paying churches will be after you.

Now is the time, then, to perfect yourself in the skills of the popular preacher. No other professional investment will return such dividends on so small a capitalization. It is a situation comparable to having gotten in on the initial stock offering of IBM or General Motors.

The first rule for the popular preacher to remember as he prepares a sermon is that style is of enormous importance while content makes little ultimate difference in the congregation's enthusiasm for one's efforts in the pulpit. About 1000 parts style to 1 part content is a good proportion.

No one cares very much what you say when you preach, so long as it is not radically controversial or disturbing. Your acceptability as a preacher depends almost wholly on how you say it. A really gifted preacher can deliver an exegesis of "Mary Had a Little Lamb" or extol the virtues of the single tax and send the congregation home in a spiritual trance, while a bumbler can bore it to death with a sensible and relevant exposition of the parable of the prodigal son.

All too few young clerics starting at the front door of their career trouble themselves to ask the question "What do my people want from a sermon?" Rather, they ask themselves "What had I ought to give my congregation when I preach?" Which is only another form of the question "What do I want to give them?"

Fundamentally, preaching at its best is one of the entertainment arts, and the successful pulpiteer will always think of himself first as an entertainer. His problem is much the same as Jack Benny's or Shelley Berman's or Mort Sahl's. He has to stand up and keep the customers interested in what he is saying or business will fall off at an alarming rate. The following chapters will examine the techniques of pulpit entertainment.

Entertain the customers

The old pros of the pulpit know that they should always aim to do three things for and to the customers (congregation) in every sermon:

1. Make them laugh
2. Make them cry
3. Make them feel religious

This does not mean that people in church should be induced to guffaw like drunks in a night club. The amenities of civilized churchgoing preclude this sort of congregational behavior. A preacher should not aim to be a belly-laugh comedian—but he should be a hearty-giggle humorist or he is unlikely to be called to a major league pastorate.

This level of skill is attained by loading the sermon with funny stories. They don't need to illustrate anything (one can always contrive to make a story fit); they just need to be funny.

The wise young clergyman, then, will early begin the habit of collecting funny stories. Buy books of them, clip them out of newspapers and magazines, paste them in scrapbooks or keep them in files. You can never have too many of them.

Let us now illustrate how to go about selecting a funny story for pulpit use. Let us suppose you are preparing a sermon on Christian missions. One of your points will likely be "The joys and advantages of being a Christian." Now when you come to this point in the sermon you can say, "Of course there are disadvantages to being a Christian. Sometimes people take advantage of the Christian's spirit of benevolence. This reminds me[1] of the story of the Jewish man who was converted to Christianity. After he was baptized and received into the church, he went home and was met at the door by his son who said, 'Pop, I need $5000 for a new sports car,' and his father gave it to him. As he came into the front room, his daughter came in and said, 'Father, I'm going to Europe and the trip will cost $5000,' so he gave it to her. As he went into the kitchen to see what was cooking, his wife said to him, 'Dear, I've ordered a new mink coat and it costs $5000.' So he gave it to her.

"Then, alone for a moment, he meditated on all this.

"'Here I've been a Christian for a half-hour,' he said to himself, 'and these damn[2] Jews have taken me for $15,000 already.'"

Here is a nearly ideal humorous sermon illustration. For one thing, it does illustrate a point more or less. (And though we have previously noted that this is by no means necessary, it is a good idea to connect up your stories to the sermon wherever possible—and it usually is.) More important, it subtly reinforces your people in one of the

---

[1] One is always "reminded" of a story in the pulpit, even though hours have been spent locating it and it is a part of the manuscript.
[2] In less sophisticated churches substitute "darn" for "damn."

prejudices to which they cling with tenacity and makes them feel comfortable about it.

You can be certain that any middle-class, standard-brand Protestant congregation is anti-Semitic. Not blatantly anti-Semitic, of course. You would get the gate in no time at all if you preached the Gerald L. K. Smith line. Also, hardly any of your good people would admit to prejudice against Jews. It isn't popular to do so, and besides everyone wants to think he is tolerant. Most of your members even know and like some individual Jewish family. But to a person they think of Jews as avaricious, selfish, grasping and quick to take advantage of the other fellow. At the same time, they feel vaguely guilty about feeling this way.

So with this illustration, you have managed to imply (a) that Jews are actually like we all think they are, and (b) if Jews would only become Christians they would immediately become generous, warmhearted and unselfish like us, and (c) the Christian religion is demonstrably superior to the Jewish religion and, by implication, to all other religions.

So in this one brief story you have succeeded in extending permission to hold a prejudice, absolved the people of their guilt over holding it,[3] and have made them feel good about being Christian because Christians are superior people. And all this has been accomplished in the most entertaining of ways—through a funny story.

You cannot hope to turn up so ideal an example of the humorous story for pulpit use every week in the year. But if you keep it in mind as a model, it will help you in your selections and remind you to make the people laugh.

Make them cry

Now we come to the art of making them cry. Of course we do not mean that actual tears must flow (although if

---

[3.] Absolution of guilt has always been one of the first functions and duties of a priest.

the custodian regularly comes upon damp discarded Kleenex when he picks up after the service, it is a heartening indication that you are consistently striking the bull's-eye). A lump in the throat and a quivering sensation in the breast, however, are quite adequate.

For making them cry, so to speak, your best bets are stories about old-fashioned virtues and values, patriotism and self-sacrifice. If you tell them properly these will always do the trick.

Let us inspect a brief example of the lump-in-the-throat story.

A poor but scholarly and conscientious preacher has a little girl who desperately wants a new dress for an important party at the home of a wealthy parishioner. Her father sadly tells her there isn't any money for a new dress (build up his pain and anguish). She can't understand it, so finally her mother takes her into her father's study, points to the rows of books and says, "Darling, here is the reason there is no money for a new dress."

The point here which is calculated to open up the tear ducts is that the little girl must give up what all little girls have as an inalienable right to possess in order that her poor, struggling father may have the tools to do the Lord's work.

The story, of course, is full of logical holes. One could just as well conclude that her father sacrificed his daughter's welfare to his passion for scholarship. Why did he need all those expensive books? Why couldn't he have sacrificed a little for his daughter's sake? If his parishioners wanted a scholarly preacher, why shouldn't they pay the freight?

But be assured that your hearers will never even think of these questions. They will only feel sad and tearful over the plight of the little girl caught in the meshes of a necessary self-denial that a high and noble end may be achieved.

This story has the added advantage of a subliminal but

persistent suggestion that the clergy bears the burden of great hidden expenses, which, you will discover, is all too true. It could easily produce a substantial book-allowance item for you in the next church budget.

You must not be too crude with the "cry stories," of course. Little Nell dying of malnutrition in the garret because Papa spends all the money at the saloon served her day, but the modern congregation, however plebeian, will not respond to it and might even chuckle—which would be disconcerting to you to say the least.

The untimely passing of a lovely young thing in the bloom of youth leaving behind a desolate and inconsolable lover is a theme with excellent possibilities so long as it is made clear that the love relationship has been entirely spiritual in nature. Turn the Lady of the Camellias into a church deaconess or a virgin schoolteacher and you will be amazed at the lachrymose response you will get.

Make them feel religious

Now we come to the problem of making them feel religious. This is the easiest of the three because it is mostly a matter of nomenclature. You need only employ a sufficient number of words and phrases which are loaded with "religious" meaning to accomplish the desired end.

For quick reference, the author here includes a brief lexicon of graded religious words and phrases. Roughly, a number one word or phrase has twice the religious punch of a number two and three times that of a number three.

LEXICON

Faith of our Fathers (1)

Bible-believing Christians (1)

Repentance (3) (Many people are not enthusiastic about repenting.)

Salvation (2) (A good word, but carries some overtones of the camp meeting.)

The Bible says (1) (Billy Graham's favorite phrase. Most congregations will believe anything you say if you precede it with this phrase.)

Christ-centered (1) (Use this often.)

Righteousness (3) (Given the lowest rating because it implies that Christians ought to behave themselves according to a standard stricter than many church members care to observe.)

God-fearing (1) (Your people aren't afraid of God, of course, but they enjoy thinking that they are.)

Serve the Lord with Gladness (1) (This has a fine biblical and literary ring to it, sounds as if you are calling for instant, forthright action, but is sufficiently vague as to require nothing at all from your hearers. Hard to beat.)

The Good Book (2) (Older members will like it, but it is a little dated for younger people.)

Sin (*or sinners*) (1) (Every sermon should include one or the other. These words conjure up images of bordellos and orgies and black lingerie—which images have an entertainment value in themselves. Your people will never connect the words with anything that middle-class white Protestants do, so you can flail away at sin and sinners to your heart's content.)

The Kingdom of God (1) (Your congregation has heard this phrase from every preacher that ever served them, so they consider it a true mark of a devout and stable minister.)

Holiness unto the Lord (1) (Not one member has a clue as to what this means but it is one of the most euphonious and soul-satisfying phrases in the lexicon.)

Heaven (1) (No preacher ever got fired for preaching about heaven so long as he made it clear that he thought everyone in his congregation would get there.)

Hell (3) (Just as well lay off this one or use it sparingly.)

These examples should suffice to give you the general idea of how to go about making your people feel religious. As a rule of thumb, rely heavily on those words and phrases which evoke pleasant religious feelings, and use with considerable economy any word which might make people uncomfortable or fidgety (which is why we warn against preaching about hell, for you would be surprised at the members of your flock who are trying to quash the suspicion that they might end up there).

Notes on noteless preaching

Let us now turn our attention to some do's and don'ts of preaching, little practical suggestions—each by itself a small thing perhaps—but put together adding up to great things for you so far as preferment in your calling is concerned.

At the top of the list of those items which you should do is this: Always preach without manuscript or notes of any kind.

Young clergymen seldom grasp the value of perfecting themselves in the "noteless" style of sermon delivery. Most of us have weak memories and feel horribly insecure without the comforting presence of a manuscript on the podium in front of us. Not one person in a thousand feels naturally inclined to this style of delivery. It is this very scarcity of noteless preachers which works to the advantage of the man who is one.

When you preach without notes, the focus of attention for the congregation is not your sermon but your performance. Since most of your listeners are paralyzed and inarticulate in front of an audience with everything they intend to say written down and before them, they are vastly amazed that anyone can stand up and talk for twenty minutes or so without visible aids to the memory, no matter what he says.

This situation obviates the need for undue concern over the content of your sermon since hardly anyone will be more than casually interested in what you say, thus lightening your preparatory labors and granting you many extra hours every week to do with what you please—hours which your less gifted brethren of the cloth will spend sweating over the manufacture of a manuscript for Sunday morning.

You may have observed already that the possession of a noteless preacher is a genuine status symbol for a church, the ecclesiastical equivalent of a chinchilla coat or recognition by the headwaiter at Le Pavillon. These confer status because they are rare, and rare status symbols cost quite a bit of money. This law operates just as surely in the ecclesiastical world as in the secular world, and a noteless preacher always commands a higher salary than even the most profound of his brethren who encumber themselves with manuscripts.

Those fortunate few congregations blessed with a noteless preacher become inordinately proud of him, and brag about him much as they brag about breaking 80 at golf or being invited to the Governor's for tea. They never comment that their preacher is learned or witty or forceful or devout or thought-provoking or inspiring. They always say, "You know, he preaches without a single note."

Also, the noteless style endears you to the extremely pious members of your flock who tend to be suspicious of written sermons on the grounds that excessive advance preparation allows insufficient opportunities for the workings of divine inspiration. The extemporaneous homily seems to them to come from the heart instead of the head, and is thus a sure sign and seal that their preacher is "spiritual."

Since the pietists are a hard-core type of group in the congregation, sticking together like scotch tape and presenting a solid front in both their enthusiasms and their dislikes, it is a group to be reckoned with. A sensitive ecclesiastical politician can always smell an impending change of pastorates by sniffing the wind near the pietists of the congregation. If the pietists are voicing criticisms of their pastors, no matter how few and mild, the cloud no larger than a man's hand has appeared on the horizon and this pastor is well advised to start looking for another job, because the pietists will eventually get him. They are as relentless as Javert. Therefore, the wise pastor will learn how to cater to this group, and noteless preaching is one of the best ways to commend himself to it. Exhaustive research by the author has failed to turn up a single case of a noteless preacher falling into disrepute with the pietists of his congregation.

A preaching program which can't miss

As you begin your career of labor for the Lord, you must keep in mind that, while the content matter of your sermons is not too important if your style is adequate, there are some types of sermons which are almost guaranteed to win enthusiastic reactions from your congregation.

If you will never forget that your beloved parishioners are primarily interested in themselves, their spiritual aches and pains, their desire for whatever they equate with happiness, their urge to succeed socially and financially, the preservation of their provincial prejudices, then you will do the bulk of your preaching on these subjects.

One eminent New York preacher whose name escapes us at the moment (Freud would probably have been able to account for our forgetfulness) has become the best-known Protestant clergyman of our generation, has made pots of money and acquired all the good things which come the way of the sensationally successful preacher simply by remembering this one simple fact. Buy his books, hear him at every opportunity, and imitate him insofar as it is possible for you to do so and you, too, will hit the ecclesiastical jackpot.

Your people, you will discover, have an insatiable appetite for sermons on how to improve themselves or solve their emotional (spiritual) problems so long as the panacea you offer them does not require them to (a) quit doing anything they like to do, (b) spend any money or (c) submit to any very rigorous or time-consuming spiritual discipline.

What you need, then, is a formula tailored and trimmed to the above specifications. The author suggests that whenever you preach a "how to use the Christian Faith to get what you want" type of sermon (and you should be preaching just such a sermon eight Sundays out of ten) it is well to rely on a formula which varies no more than the rotation of the earth. The formula is this: Whether the sermon deals with the problem of loneliness, frustration, marital felicity, getting ahead in one's business or whatever, the solution to the problem is always:

(a) a catchy, easily remembered Bible verse (variable with each sermon according to the topic)

(b) a simple, sunny little prayer to repeat as needed (also variable, as above)

(c) an exhortation to have faith (this item is invariable. You don't have to be specific about faith—in fact, it is better if you are not specific—just urge faith. Faith in faith is the best-selling item in your line of goods you will discover. There is very little sales resistance to it).

One obstacle you will need to overcome in training yourself to preach Sunday after Sunday on these "helping yourself through the Gospel" themes is the immense boredom you will suffer. Since you will be preaching essentially the same sermon nearly every Sunday, changing only the title, the text and the illustrations, you will find it difficult to convince yourself that your congregation will not be bored too. But it won't, and this you must accept as an article of your homiletical faith. No one has yet come up with a satisfactory explanation for this phenomenon. It is just a fact of life. Trust it and act on it.

The remaining 20 per cent of your preaching can be devoted, for the most part, to sermons for special occasions. These should be keyed to our more important national holidays. Many youthful clergymen, inspired no doubt by the highest and most pious motives, begin their careers by using the Christian calendar as a guide for their preaching. But the wise ones quickly discard this antiquated practice. The only days in the so-called church year which merit a special sermon are Christmas and Easter—and these merit it because they have evolved into important national, commercial holidays rather than for any vestigial religious significance still clinging to them.

Following is a month-by-month listing of the special days you will want to observe from the pulpit along with suggested themes for the day.

JANUARY

First Sunday—New Year's Day sermon. Topic: "Twelve Joyous Months With Jesus."

FEBRUARY

Sunday nearest Washington's birthday. Topic: "Faithful to the Faith of Our Nation's Founder." (This may be changed on alternate years to the Sunday nearest Lincoln's birthday. It involves only a slight change in the topic, which might be "Faithful to the Faith of Our Greatest President." The sermon can be substantially the same.)

MARCH

No particularly important special day unless Easter falls in March.

APRIL

Easter Sunday (usually). Topic: "Looking Forward to a Good, Old-Fashioned Heaven." (Do not forget to give the Easter-only churchgoers a thorough lacing for their failure to show up the rest of the year. This gives the regulars a sense of their own righteousness and spiritual superiority, and the Easter-only crowd expects to catch it from the preacher because they always have. They will not mend their ways, of course, but they hardly feel they have been to church if you fail to flay them.)

MAY

Second Sunday—Mother's Day. Topic: "Our Mother's Faith."

JUNE

Third Sunday—Father's Day. Topic: "Faith of Our Fathers."

JULY

Sunday nearest Fourth of July (might fall on last Sunday in June). Topic: "God's Chosen People." (Stressing, of course, that America and Americans are God's examples of what He expects other nations and other peoples to be like. This sermon may also be used at American Legion rallies and other patriotic occasions. It is a sure-fire hit.)

AUGUST

These are the dog days for church attendance. No special days. Better take your vacation in August.

SEPTEMBER

Sunday nearest Labor Day (could be last Sunday in August). Topic: "God's Labor Laws." (Point out that the laboring man needs to get back to the old-fashioned values of an honest day's work for an honest wage, and gratitude for the enterprising and risk-taking capitalist who makes his job possible. Express sympathy and concern for the good workmen of America caught in the evil grip of organized labor. Since you are likely to have few members of labor unions and lots of employers in your congregation, this will be one of the most popular sermons of the year.)

OCTOBER

Last Sunday—Reformation Sunday. Topic: "The Menace of an Alien Religion." (Reformation day isn't much of a special occasion in our churches, but it does afford an opportunity to whack the Roman Catholics. Since there is a mood of tolerance in the air, what with the late President Kennedy and the late Pope John, care

must be taken to attack the still unpopular aspects of
Roman Catholicism—the political aims of the Vatican,
the mumbo-jumbo of its priestcraft, that sort of thing.)

NOVEMBER

Sunday before Thanksgiving. Topic: "God's Blessing
Means God's Approval." (The theme here is that God
has blessed America beyond the blessings of any other
land, which means that God likes us best.)

DECEMBER

Christmas Sunday—Topic: "The Babe from Heaven."
(There is simply no way to preach an unpopular sermon when you have a baby, motherhood, heaven,
humble shepherds and adoring wise men to talk about.
Stick to the pageantry of Christmas. Beware of explor-
ing the meaning of the Advent very much beneath the
surface aspects of the story, for this can get you into
trouble.)

Had this book been written a few years ago, the author
would have issued an iron-bound injunction against any
preaching which attempts to relate the Gospel to contem-
porary social issues. Nothing subtracts from the market-
ability of a preacher so much as having the label "liberal"
pinned on him. Not many of us invite attacks on our theological orthodoxy these days because 99–44/100 of any modern
standard-brand congregation is so theologically untutored
that it wouldn't be able to recognize a heretic. It has no way
of distinguishing between theological orthodoxy and heresy.
But it is quick to spot any slight leaning toward liberal
social views in its pastor. Heresy today is social rather than
theological, and every congregation has its self-appointed
Torquemadas anxious to oil the rack or heat up the fires
around the stake.

It would be best, therefore, if the preacher could avoid
entirely any reference to any subject which has a side to it
capable of being construed as "liberal." The author can
remember when church life had a lovely, serene, otherworldly flavor to it because preachers did not concern them-

selves with temporal problems. But this day has disappeared because we now live in unhappy times in which every newspaper brings tidings of some social problem which directly involves religion, the church and the faith and which forces us to make some kind of response.

It is, in fact, a decided advantage to you to be known as a fearless and forthright and prophetic pulpit voice—so long as you can achieve this reputation without being thought liberal. So you will have to venture out into the choppy and shoal-filled waters of preaching on social issues. There is no avoiding it, or the author would counsel you to do so.

The danger of being specific

This, then, is the most dangerous part of the preaching ministry. But if you will follow three simple principles, you can mitigate the dangers of shipwreck.

The first principle is this: Never be specific as to the Christian position on any burning social issue of the day.

For example, if you feel compelled by current events to preach on racial segregation, never, repeat, never, suggest that integration is the Christian solution. In fact, eschew the term "integration" entirely. It is far too specific.

The points you will want to make in this sermon will go something like this:

1. Extremism in racial matters is the chief evil.
2. The colored people ought to reflect on the great strides forward they have made and not be too impatient for too much too soon.
3. Brotherhood and Christian love will point the way. "You can't legislate love" is an excellent phrase to use here. (Since the congregation will define "Brotherhood" and "Christian love" to mean a kind of vague good will toward colored people so long as they stay in their place, they will take no offense at this.)

The problem here is to avoid any suggestion that white Protestant Christians have been at any point remiss in their attitudes or actions, and at the same time outline a solution which involves new attitudes and actions (since any idiot can reason that if what we have always done isn't working, we had darn well better think up something else).

This is a delicate but not insoluble dilemma for the preacher. The way out is to keep handy a set of non-specific words and phrases which allow the members of the congregation to fill in their own meaning. "Brotherhood" and "Christian love" have already been mentioned. It is always a good idea to urge your people to employ more of "the spirit of Christ" in the solution to social tensions, since hardly any of them know what this means but practically all of them think they do.

What you have working for you here is the average American citizen's touching faith in simple solutions to vast and complex problems. And people who believe that a balanced budget or bombing Cuba or a Republican administration would solve the problems of the nation and the world will have no difficulty believing that your non-specific phrases are clear Christian answers and that you are therefore a keen and courageous preacher.

A second principle to follow in preaching on social issues is to preach on problems which are as remote as possible from your community. You can denounce the government of South Africa with all the vigor at your command, but be careful about denouncing political corruption in your own city, because some of your good members might be involved. Criticize to your heart's content the Godless New York stage, but don't knock the local movie house, because someone in your congregation may be leasing it to the operator.

The third principle, and perhaps the one of pristine value to you in preaching on social issues, is to reserve your righteous indignation for those questions on which there is no substantial disagreement among your members.

As this is written, the Supreme Court ruling on prayer in the public schools is getting a lot of attention in the press. Since most of your people have been led to believe by the papers they read that the Supreme Court is systematically undermining the American way of life, they will welcome several sermons on "this atheistic decision." This issue should be good for several years yet. But by far the safest social problem on which the preacher may take an unequivocal position is the temperance question. You are aware, of course, that in the newspeak of the temperance movement temperance doesn't mean temperance. It means total abstinence from the use of beverage alcohol.

Your congregation is made up of members who advocate temperance and members who drink without apology, the proportions varying with the size, sophistication and urban or rural character of your community. But both groups expect the preacher to trot out a temperance sermon every so often in addition to frequent blasts on the subject as a subpoint in other sermons. The temperance people love to hear you lambaste booze, and the drinkers are not offended by it because they understand that this just goes along with your job. A preacher who doesn't preach temperance sermons is as unthinkable as a Frenchman who frowns on love. This is the one social issue which involves no danger whatever, no matter how violent your denunciation.[4]

If you understand your people, their hopes and fears and prides and prejudices (and every truly successful pastor does understand these things), then all you need to do to be a highly regarded pulpit man is to tell them what you know they want to hear. After all, they are badgered and buffeted by worldly cares six days a week, and they need a sanctuary from all this on Sunday. They should be able to come to the Lord's house when the sweet church bells chime secure in the knowledge that they will find it here. They should come anticipating a jolly, sprightly, positive, enter-

[4.] The author knows of three churches which realize a considerable amount of annual income from the leasing of property on which alcoholic beverages are dispensed. Yet the pastors of these churches continue to preach anti-booze sermons with, apparently, the complete approval of their congregations.

taining, non-controversial homily from their beloved man of God, aware that no discouraging or disturbing word will be spoken from your pulpit.

If your good people can count on this kind of preaching from you, you can count on their heartfelt appreciation expressed in their continuing affection, fulsome praise, a solid reputation as a fine pulpit man, and more tangible evidences of gratitude in the form of salary increases, better housing, and maybe a trip abroad for you and your wife with all expenses paid. Your true reward (apart from a perfectly legitimate joy in your professional success) will be, of course, the knowledge that you have served the Lord by comforting his people—and this is the knowledge which maketh glad the heart.

THE ADMINISTRATION OF A CHURCH, WHICH IS

A POLITE PHRASE FOR RAISING MONEY

IV

In an earlier chapter, it was averred that we would be coming to the treatment of those skills and talents which really pay off for the preacher in charge of a congregation. We have now arrived at that promised point.

A congregation is fundamentally a business enterprise. No one mentions this rather obvious fact to the ambitious young theologs during their period of professional training. When you were required to write a paper on "The Theology of the Church" for Dr. Van Fuzz's course Christian Doctrine II, you probably defined a church as "the gathered community of Faith" or "the Body of Christ" or employed some other equally elegant theological phrase.

This was the thing to do, of course, for had you defined it as "a business enterprise" the ancient and learned doctor would have flunked you without turning a single straggly gray hair. The author does not mean to imply that such definitions are wrong or that they are not useful on occasion. They are in the nature of ideals, of beautiful goals to move toward if you can fathom what they mean. They have their place (in learned papers mostly). But do not confuse them with reality. Above all, do not plunge out of seminary and into your first pastorate heart and mind aquiver with the solemn thought "I am now in charge of a community of faith." To do so is to invite professional disaster at the very first stage of your career.

What you are in charge of is not a community of faith but a business enterprise. Your seminary professors do not understand this. Seminary professors are very short on knowledge of how a local church operates, few of them ever having been pastors, but your bishop understands it. The trustees or board or vestry or session of your church understands it. Your brother clergymen understand it. And your wife, who must cope with the frequently grim facts of parsonage economics, understands it. (You may be amazed at the rapidity with which she grasps the essential nature of the church.)

Too many otherwise promising young clerics are encouraged to minimize the business-management side of the pastoral ministry because it is so seldom mentioned. But the fact that it isn't mentioned, or treated lightly, by even the tightest member of your board of deacons should indicate to you not its unimportance, but only that good and sensitive Christian people don't like to be reminded of it. Or, to put it plainly, there is a conspiracy of silence as to the commercial aspects of the church. This, it seems to the author, is the part of wisdom. After all, our Lord drove the money-changers out of the temple. And there is something unbecoming about crass materialism in the house of God.

The knowledgeable clergyman, then, will co-operate in this conspiracy of silence. If he doesn't, he lays himself open to the charge of "worldliness" or "lack of spirituality" which will severely damage the public image of the cloth as a profession and cause the sweet Christian souls under his care to be on their guard against any proposal or program he may suggest lest it cost them money.

Experience will teach you that it is seldom necessary to make public mention of church business and finance. On those rare occasions when it is necessary, remember to avoid the use of the word "money." Speak of "bringing the tithes into the storehouse" or "the Lord's business."[1] It sounds so much better. It doesn't jar or grate on religious sensibilities. However, though you will seldom mention money and the church, you will learn to think about it all the time. It will become (if you intend to make your mark) the fundamental fact of your professional life.

"Church administration" is simply a refined term for "raising money." It involves, of course, all sorts of activities—committee meetings, publicity, promotion, budget preparation, building supervision, public relations, etc., but it is all related to keeping your church solvent.

European churchmen from lands where the church derives its support from taxes are amazed that people will voluntarily contribute enough money to finance religion. What they fail to understand is that extracting all this cash requires clergymen who combine business acumen, a good working knowledge of human nature, and the persuasiveness of a circus pitchman.

The theology of church finance

If the author had his way, he would include as a part of the core curriculum of every school of divinity several courses on "The Theology of Church Finance." For public relations purposes it would be wise to call these courses "The Theology of Christian Stewardship." But for the sake of clarity, we have used "Church Finance." Such studies should certainly take precedence over the pursuit of musty old biblical languages which will never be of any conceivable use in the parish ministry, and should have as many if not more hours devoted to them as New Testament exegesis or church history. As we have noted, the vast majority of your pastoral cares will have to do with money, not Bible or history or

[1.] See the author's article "The Effective Employment of the Sacred Euphemism in Raising the Church's Annual Budget," which was included in *The Compendium of Practical Theology*, now unfortunately out of print.

Christian instruction. Why not, then, devote the bulk of your training to those skills which will be your best and most important resource during the years ahead?

Though the restrictions of space do not permit here an exhaustive treatment of "The Theology of Church Finance" there is, so far as the author knows, no authoritative work on the subject extant,[2] so we will include a brief outline of the theology.

Fortunately there is no need to manufacture a Theology of Church Finance. It already exists, embedded in the body of Christian doctrine which has been venerated for centuries and thus has the authority and power of tradition behind it. This eliminates the necessity of establishing and defending your assumptions since they are already established and to question them is to commit the sin of heresy. Your good people would never even consider the possibility that accepted Christian doctrine could be wrong.

The Theology of Church Finance actually has only two cardinal doctrines, both drawn from the spiritual well of Christian orthodoxy.

The first doctrine and the keystone in the arch of our Theology of Church Finance is the "Doctrine of Original Sin."

Now the author is aware that this time-honored and excellent doctrine, which is stated so beautifully in the Genesis story of the fall of man, has in our time been treated rather lightly in the liberal seminaries. There has been, instead, an emphasis on man's essential goodness, his potential for righteousness. You may have been taught that if we can only give people enough education and inside plumbing, the Kingdom of God will automatically arrive. This, of course, makes for very popular preaching since most of the people you preach to have an education and inside plumbing, so they are led to believe that the Kingdom has already

[2.] This is quite understandable. You can't find any published information on "The Philosophy of Fee Setting for Medical Doctors" either.

arrived for them, that they are safely within the gates.

In fact, there is no reason why you can't use this approach for your preaching theology. If it comforts your people and makes them feel good, you have successfully performed a pastoral duty. Actually, there is something to be said for making your flock feel good through your sermons, because this makes them feel good toward the church and prepares them spiritually for the financial appeal. But many young preachers who are otherwise able and show real promise make the fatal error of carrying this positive, pleasant theology over into the hard, practical business of raising money. Then, true to their doctrine, they stress "Christian steward-ship" and "giving gladly" and that sort of thing. Then they wonder why they have an eternal struggle with the church budget.

The reason is actually quite apparent. People can give fifty cents gladly—they are glad to feel they have given, and they are glad to have gotten the glad feeling at such a bar-gain price. But if you expect to extract any real money from them, you have to offer a motive with considerably more horsepower than simple gladness. This motive is contained in the Doctrine of Original Sin. And just in case you don't have a firm grasp of the doctrine, perhaps a brief explana-tion will prove helpful.

Briefly, and forgetting for the moment the formal biblical background for the doctrine, it says that every man is by nature predisposed to seek in everything his own selfish ends; that he will always look after his own interests first. It also holds that every man is aware of this flaw in his nature even if that awareness lurks in the murky depths of his subconscious. It has to be this way, of course. For if a fellow didn't know, either consciously or unconsciously, that he is a sinner, he wouldn't be a sinner.

Strange as it seems, the greatest thing that ever came down the pike so far as the hard-pressed parish pastor is concerned, is the psychology of Sigmund Freud. Freud taught us about guilt and put his message across in a way

that preachers had never been able to manage. He made
guilt fashionable. Guilt is "in." Freud was an agnostic, of
course, but then God works in mysterious ways His wonders
to perform, and for purposes of money raising (and let us
put it in capital letters so that it will be emblazoned on
your memory) NOTHING IS HALF SO EFFECTIVE AS THE EX-
PLOITATION OF YOUR PARISHIONERS' GUILT FEELINGS!!!

Perhaps it never occurred to you that the clean, sweet-
smelling, well-behaved members of your congregation are
really sinners. But depend on the absolute accuracy of the
Doctrine of Original Sin. They are.

The pallid sins of nice people

It is true that not many of them are spectacular sinners.
Their transgressions tend to be petty, unimaginative, and
thoroughly middle-class. But they are sinners all the same,
and while they pretend that they are not, they know it.

Very few of your good people pursue sin in the form of
wine, women and song. This is because such pursuit is in-
convenient, time-consuming and expensive. Most of all, it
reduces one's effectiveness as a money maker. And the
average middle-class white Protestant much prefers building his bank account and collecting status symbols to in-
dulging himself in the so-called pleasures of the flesh.[3]

Now this is a fact which you need to keep in mind at all
times, and especially when planning the annual budget
drive or building-fund campaign or any other type of
financial appeal. Scorching your people for the rough,
rowdy, boisterous, bold, bawdy sins will bring very little
cash into the till. This kind of talk just makes them feel
smug and superior. Hardly anyone you will minister to ever
even thought of sinning with abandon. Nice people don't do

[3.] Do not neglect to imply, though, that you know this kind of hanky-
panky goes on. Even in the most proper congregation you will snag
an errant soul now and then who wonders ruefully how you got
onto him.

these things, and happily for us, the church has progressed to the place where it serves nice people almost exclusively. We have come a long way from the early days of the church when Christianity did not appeal very much to the nice people of the time and members had to be recruited from the rough, unlettered and profane classes. How much easier it would have been for our dear Lord had he been able to deal with the merchant and banking levels of society instead of with fishermen and petty tax collectors and the like. But, as noted, above, denouncing the sins which nice people do not commit only makes them feel spiritually superior. And the man who is encouraged to feel spiritually superior generally ends up by revising downward the amount he had planned to give to the church.

However, nice people are quite vulnerable at the point of their prosperity. The average man really has a rather low opinion of himself, even when he covers it with bluster and bragging. He is astounded to find himself living in a forty-thousand-dollar home, driving two automobiles and belonging to the country club. He wants you to believe that all this is tangible evidence of his wit, energy and general superiority. But in his heart he knows, though he may never acknowledge it even to himself, that it is mostly luck. Also, he lives uneasily with the information that he has managed to squeeze out of society far more than his contribution to society is worth. And since his security, the structure of his personality, and everything he holds precious in life is squarely dependent on these lovely results of what he pretends is his personal superiority but what he believes to be his good fortune, he is haunted by one horrible, nightmarish fear—that somehow these things will disappear as easily as they came. This is why so many of your people support Robert Welch or Billy James Hargis. They are wildly enthusiastic about anyone who promises to ward off those who want to take it away. In short, your average man is prosperous and he feels guilty about it. The astute pastor, then, will learn how to remind his people (there are a thousand ways) of how greatly the Lord has blessed them and that these blessings are far beyond anything they deserve.

This has the advantage of being good, sound, demonstrable biblical teaching plus being a solid, practical approach to prying out of them the money you need to carry on the Lord's work. Couple this with the subtle but frequent suggestion that "the Lord giveth and the Lord taketh away" and that he might do just that, and you have created the ideal atmosphere for maximum results from a church finance campaign. There is, however, one exception to this rule— this appeal won't work with people of inherited wealth. They are accustomed to having money and assume it is the will of God that they should have it. However, be comforted by two thoughts: (1) You won't have many such people in your flock and (2) nothing else works with them either.

The peace which passeth understanding

Creating in your good, prosperous flock feelings of guilt (or, more accurately, bringing to the surface of their awareness the guilt feelings they already have but which they attempted to dispose of by cramming them into the subconscious) is not sufficient to get the job done, though. You must also utilize the second cardinal doctrine in our Theology of Church Finance.

The official name of this doctrine is "Salvation by Works." It means, as you know if you did not neglect your courses in systematic theology, that God permits us to earn His favor by our performance of enough approved good acts or deeds (works). It also involves the avoidance of those activities and indulgences which the Almighty supposedly frowns on.

Since nearly everyone is disinclined to exhaust themselves performing all the good works they suspect they need to perform in order to be acceptable to God and insure that their names are inscribed in the heavenly reservation lists; and since we all harbor guilt feeling for real or imagined transgressions, there is a need for "a more excellent way," a relatively painless method of obtaining the desired spiritual benefits.

Our Roman Catholic friends understand this quite well, and early in the history of the church grasped the immense spiritual possibilities of the universal need to earn favor with God. They formulated the doctrine of Salvation by Works, and included the payment of appropriate sums of money to the church in the list of acceptable good works. It must now be apparent to you that your problem is to "Protestant-ize" this fine and beneficial Roman doctrine. What is required is the encouragement of the conviction that expiation of sin, peace of mind and the kind smile of the Almighty are available to those whose generosity toward the church is notable and consistent.

The author is one who believes a little humor and levity associated with the demanding tasks of the parish ministry is a good thing among professionals, so the following limerick is offered to make our point, to help fix it in your mind, and perhaps bring a bit of fun into an otherwise grim undertaking.

> There was a church deacon named Linn
> Who succumbed to original sin.
> When his guilt became onerous
> He wrote a check generous
> It's now a state of grace that he's in.

Now the question is bound to arise in your mind, "How can we encourage our good Protestant people to purchase their salvation when the chief doctrine of the Protestant Reformation was 'Justification (or Salvation) by Faith'?" How can we tell them that the good work of generous financial support of the church will catch God's attention, merit His approval, and prompt Him to punch the blessing button and pour out on them His richest favors when our official theology holds that not only do we not need to make ourselves acceptable to God, but that we can't do it no matter how hard we try? At first glance this would seem to be an insurmountable obstacle. But it is not so difficult as you might suppose.

Most of your faithful flock has never even heard of the Protestant doctrine of Justification by Faith. And even the minority which has heard of it has never connected it with themselves or real life.

Since we live in a world where everything has a price, where anything good has to be fought for, struggled for, sacrificed for, it is inconceivable to your people that even God is going to give them anything for free. They feel it deep in their hearts that they must somehow merit the divine forgiveness before it can be bestowed on them. They know with a primitive, sub-rational intuition that cannot be shaken by a contrary doctrine which has only the Bible to back it up that they must accomplish their own atonement.

The understanding pastor, then, will not confuse his good people with a lot of abstruse theology, however correct. Especially he will not do this when the end result of its acceptance would be, in all likelihood, a drastic reduction in his church's cash income. Rather, any clergyman with a truly pastoral heart will covet for all of his people the peace which passeth understanding. And if this can be had by a simple monetary transaction, why force them to accept and understand a difficult doctrine? As shepherds we desire that the sheep under our care shall be spiritually blessed and comforted—and if a little fleecing will produce the desired results, then who is to say that this is not good? We should rejoice in a situation in which everyone wins.

It may be that you are offended by the thought of encouraging a doctrine which runs counter to orthodox Protestant theology. If so, be comforted by the knowledge that even if you preached every Sunday on the teaching of God's free grace, you would discover that your people would be extremely reluctant to abandon the belief in the efficacy of good works to justify (square them) before the Almighty.

The reason for this reluctance is attributable, in part, to the fact that many of them have tried to be good, have abstained from carousing around and in general avoided enjoying life overmuch because they have thought or been told that this is how God wanted it. Thus, if you tell them that what they have tried so hard to achieve is freely available as a gift, you devalue the currency of their virtue. If they have the wit to carry this teaching to its logical end, they cannot avoid the conclusion that God loves the bum in the gutter just as much as He loves the sanitary, inhibited church member. This produces amazement followed rapidly by anger and hostility. They will be angry at the thought of the wasted years spent behaving themselves when it hasn't bought them anything after all. And then they become hostile toward the one who brought them this information, which is you. And hostile church members are nothing but trouble for the pastor.

You must never forget that the peaceful, happy church is the true community of faith. It makes life more pleasant for the pastor, it attracts new members, and it has a much higher stewardship (financial) potential than the quarrelsome congregation. One of the main goals of your pastoral administration, then, is to achieve and preserve a state of tranquillity in your church. Since Christians, from the early days of the faith, have shown a regrettable tendency to fuss and fight among themselves, this is no simple problem. However, a clever, tactful, courteous, thick-skinned minister can calm the most cantankerous of congregations. Here are a few hints to help you in this enterprise of Christian love.

Fundamental to success here is your self-image as the chief executive officer of the Lord's corporation. Our experience has led us to the conclusion that the pastor who thinks of himself as the manager of a private club is likely to outdistance his competitors in the race for clerical honors and pastoral eminence.

A club manager knows that membership and participation in the club is voluntary, so it is up to him to make it the kind of organization people want to belong to. The best way to accomplish this is to make membership in the club a status symbol.

Private clubs, of course, are able to achieve this by a policy of excluding from membership those who would, were they to be admitted, detract from the image of an organization belonged to only by those who already have status. No one wants to join anything which their Chinese laundryman or colored garbage collector can join too. So private clubs do not admit such persons to membership, good people though they may be.

A church, naturally, cannot operate in just this manner. Theoretically anyone who wishes to may join a Christian church. We aren't supposed to exclude anyone. In practice, though, it works about the same way as in the private club. The trick is to load your membership with enough of one kind of people so that other kinds of people will not ask to join.

The status church

You will discover that in each community there will be one or two "status churches" to which people from the better levels of society gravitate.[4] You are indeed fortunate if your church happens to be one of them. It takes a long time to build a church into a status symbol, and when it has become one it is next to impossible to knock it out of this class.

Some enthusiastic young pastors have foolishly tried to shove their churches up the status ladder by stressing excellent preaching, sound and attractive worship, and high-grade educational programs. This won't work. The author knows one church where the preaching is deadly dull, the worship a hodgepodge, the educational program a quarter of a century out of date, and the architecture of the building gloomy and depressing. Yet it rolls along, year after

4. It is quite simple to spot the status churches in any community. Just observe what happens when a new doctor or well-to-do lawyer moves to town. The status churches go after them like hungry tigers chasing a tasty young gazelle. The winning church will gloat, and the loser or losers will try to hide their chagrin.

year, picking up a hog's share of the affluent and privileged newcomers to the community. This is because it already has a hog's share of the affluent and privileged residents of the community.

This church has come to its present enviable and well-nigh impregnable position by following for many years now a carefully selective policy of evangelism. It is aggressive in seeking out new members—but only in those sections of town where the kind of people it wants are likely to live.

When a newcomer arrives (in the right part of town) the moving van has hardly unloaded before representatives of this church are at the door. After the usual exchange of pleasantries, the visitors say, "Look, we know you belong to another denomination, but in our town this doesn't mean much. People of your station in life here nearly always join our church." The new people are smart enough, as a rule, to check around before committing themselves. But they soon discover that the church's representatives have given them the straight goods. The appeal is almost irresistible, so they join.

The author commends this church's example as a guide for you as you struggle to put a shining public image on your congregation. Remember—if you can get enough of the right kind of people into your church you have it made.

Since your pastoral experience is limited you may be uncertain as to the grading and evaluation of prospective members. So that you may be spared the natural mistakes of youth and inexperience you will find below a list of the common categories of church members accompanied by a number for each, which is the value scale index. Thus, a member in the number ten category (the highest possible rating) is worth twice as much to your congregation as a status builder as a number five category.

It is impossible, of course, to be entirely accurate in an abstract scale. Personality, amount of wealth, degree of success in business or profession, etc., complicate the evaluation process, but if you master our index, you won't go far wrong.

STATUS VALUE SCALE INDEX

Old, aristocratic family (Without a few of these you are fighting a losing battle so far as status is concerned)	10
Millionaire (any kind) (assign a value of 9 if multimillionaire)	8
Medical Doctor (successful specialist)	7
Medical Doctor (general practitioner)	6
Lawyer (corporation and tax)	6
Lawyer (criminal, divorce, etc.)	5
Businessman (owns own business but not a millionaire)	7
Businessman (top-level management)	7
Businessman (owner of modest concern, middle-management, etc.)	5
Teacher (college with Ph.D.)	4
Teacher (college with M.A.)	2
Teacher (public school—administrative level)	3
Teacher (public school—high school)	2
Teacher (public school—grade school)	1
Musician, actor, or artist (unless "big name"—in which case assign value of 7 to 9)	2
Undertaker (successful—owns business)[5]	7

5. Make every effort to cultivate successful undertakers. More people than you imagine leave it up to him to select the clergyman for a family funeral, so he is in a position to throw several hundred dollars a year your way in fees—which he will do if he likes you and your services are short. Also, he talks to a lot of people and if he speaks highly of you, it will do you a lot of good. People respect an undertaker's opinion on preachers.

Undertaker (employee status, embalmer)	1
Osteopath	3
Chiropractor	1
Dentist (orthodontist)	6
Dentist (general practice)	5
Clerks, stenographers, business-machine operators (white-collar) (These are good people, no doubt, but they confer no status on the organization)	0
Factory Workers (supervisory level) (see explanation in above category)	0
Factory Workers (hourly rates)	—1
Day laborers (outdoor type)	—2
Colored people (unless from wealthy South American, Oriental, or Indian classes—which is unlikely)	
South American—light skin	—3
South American—dark skin	—7
Oriental—Japanese (except in California)	—3
Oriental—Chinese	—5
American Negro—light skin	—7
American Negro—dark skin	—10+

The above index is not exhaustive, but is sufficiently representative to enable you to assign any category not included its proper index number.

The able clergyman can, by the use of the index, portion out his pastoral time and efforts so as to obtain maximum return. For example, since an ordinary millionaire (not multi) carries an index of eight and a college professor (with Ph.D.) carries an index of four, one millionaire is worth—to your church's status image—two college professors.[6] Therefore, you may legitimately spend twice as much time in the pastoral cultivation of a millionaire as you would devote to a college professor.

Or, if you are after two medical doctors, one a specialist and one in general practice, a quick reference to the index shows you that a general practitioner is only six-sevenths as valuable to you as the specialist, and indicates in which direction you should weight your efforts.

Picking the right Negro

When we come to those categories assigned a minus quantity, we have a delicate problem, because the minus index measures the effort you must make to keep these people out of your church.

Let's take the extreme example. Suppose a very dark-skinned American Negro begins attending your services and there is, in your opinion, a real danger that he will ask to join. This is an ever-present possibility in these days of racial change and unrest. It could easily happen in your church and you must be prepared for the day when the problem overtakes you.

It would seem best for you to handle this exigency by doing nothing about it yourself. Rather, have a word with a trusted layman—a faithful usher, perhaps, or some other member outstanding for his tact and air of friendliness and good will. You can suggest to the layman that he have a word with the colored brother some Sunday after service. He might say, "George," (all Negro men expect to be called George) "I was talking to the pastor of the African Methodist Church (or the Mount Pisgah Baptist Church, or some

[6.] College professors, as a class, are susceptible to intellectual pride, and carp about the sermons more than any other category of members. They want you to quote Kierkegaard, Tillich and John Dewey. A preacher can't stand too many of them in the congregation. On the other hand, the average millionaire can't tell whether a sermon is good or bad, so there is no limit on the number of millionaires you can use.

other colored church) recently and happened to mention that you were attending our church. And he said to me, 'Yes, and I wish he would come down here and help us out. You have a fine, strong church and we have such a struggle to keep going. He could do so much more for the Lord with us. Besides, he would be happier with his own kind. You tell him I said that, will you?'"

A kind, considerate approach such as this, with no race prejudice, no rude suggestion that he isn't wanted should take care of the matter nicely. We must always exhibit a Christian spirit when dealing with these touchy situations.

Some of our more progressive and farsighted pastors, though, are using a different approach to the problem. They contend that it is a genuine asset, in fact almost a necessity to have a Negro member of your church these days. One of the most successful men in the author's circle of clerical acquaintances says (when speaking privately, of course), "Every church needs to have a pet nigger." And while we wouldn't want something like this said so crudely (in public) he may be right.

The idea is that one Negro member works for you and makes your church look liberal, decent, Christian in attitude, and integrated. Your author is still a bit dubious about so bold a step, though, because it entails all sorts of risks. To mention only one, it might encourage the idea that your church actually wants and welcomes any and all Negroes who care to join. This, as you immediately perceive, would be disastrous if colored people in any significant numbers took advantage of your good will.

My advice to any young, ambitious pastor would be to step very carefully here. Being young and open-minded you may be several steps ahead of your good people in your racial attitudes. After all, you don't want to force your attitudes on your people. You want to lead them gently, shepherd them carefully. And this takes time.

Should you decide to take on a Negro member for the reasons stated above, make certain that you pick the right kind. Avoid at all costs the educated, professional, superior type of colored man who is a pace setter in the Negro community. Where he leads others follow.

The very best kind, for your purposes, is a coal-black, poor, semiliterate Negro bachelor, the "Old Black Joe" type. He is no threat whatever to any of your people (a Negro schoolteacher, for example, would be better educated than some of your staunch members and they would resent this bitterly). And he would remind them of the days when racial relations were clearly defined and tranquil, not ambiguous and tension-filled as they are in our present society. In short, he would be looked on with affection as a pet. He would be coddled, protected and prized. And he would not encourage other Negroes to follow him because they would be a threat to his privileged position.

How to handle committees

Let us turn now to the problems which will confront you as you seek to implement your policies and programs through the internal administrative structure of your church.

The ambitious young divine wading into his first parish is often confused by the abundance of church committees through which he is supposed to carry on the work of his ministry. There is a committee for the promotion of missions, a committee on music, a committee on ushering, a committee on social relations, a committee on worship, a committee or board of Christian education, a house committee, a parsonage committee, a pulpit committee, a committee on finance, a benevolence committee, an interchurch relations committee, an evangelism committee, a committee to promote (raise money for) the denominational colleges of the area, a committee to promote (raise money for) the denominational hospitals and/or orphans' homes and homes for the aged, a committee on holy communion, an altar guild, a board of trustees or vestry, various committees of the ladies' organizations, and above all these an official board or session which is supposed to have final authority on all matters of internal administration.

Nothing you learned in seminary has prepared you for this. Seminary professors are as baffled by the purpose, function and use of local church committees as you are, so they skip this part of instruction in administration. And unless you are forewarned you may actually attempt to put these committees to work—or, what is worse, try to carry on your administration through them.

Calculate, for example, the drain on your time if your parish has thirty committees (a modest estimate—the number is often much higher than this) and each committee were to meet every month. Your only free nights would be in those months which have thirty-one days. Also, were all these committees active it would tax the resources of IBM's most efficient electronic computer to keep track of what they were doing. It is quite beyond the capacities of even the brightest clergyman to handle such assignments.

It is, of course, entirely unnecessary for you to attempt such a formidable task. What you must understand is that the committee structure of a church was never intended to be used. It is strictly for window dressing, to give the appearance of a democratically operated organization, or to use a more felicitous phrase, it exists for the purposes of public relations—nothing more.

The folklore of American church life has as one of its most sacred tenets the belief that the way to create a loyal church member is to give him a job to do. This is a part of our activist faith, and it is, to be sure, an excellent part for it has produced the most lively, busy and high-powered army of the Lord ever known. But it is obviously impossible to keep everyone in your church busy, or to keep even a significant fraction of your members busy. So the committee system was devised to give the appearance of everyone in the church feverishly engaged in church work.

It will soon become abundantly plain to you that it is not desirable to have very many of your good people mixing into the internal affairs of the church. For one thing, most laymen—stalwart Christians though they may be—are only mildly interested in church work, most of which is a deadly bore. For another thing, the average man in the pew is incapable of running anything and would only foul up the operation were he permitted any real authority in the handling of the church's affairs. But he likes to think he carries weight in the solemn assemblies of the ecclesiastical organization. So the thing to do is to put him on a committee (which has been created for the single purpose of having a place to put him) and he will be content.

One should never reduce the number of committees in the church structure. The author, who modestly lays claim to some skill in administration, has always followed the practice of creating several new committees shortly after unpacking his bags in a new parish. It is also well to make the purpose of the newly created committees so obscure that the people will be unable to fathom it. Thus they will assume that in your experience and wisdom you have perceived a need they did not know existed, that you are plugging a yawning gap in their church's organization. Such a procedure will quickly establish you as a hot-shot administrator, a real go-getter. You may even be told, "Reverend, you have missed your calling. Why, with your administrative ability you could make a million in business." This is the highest compliment a layman can pay you—indeed, it is the highest compliment he can conceive of paying anyone.

The men to cultivate

Even the clergyman with relatively modest intellectual equipment will learn, after a few years of parish experience, that there are only two committees in the church organization which are of any real importance. These are, by whatever particular name they are called in your denomination, the pulpit committee and the finance committee. They are important because they are the committees which (1) control your tenure and (2) set your salary. No amount of thought, trouble, care or cultivation is too much to expend on selecting and maintaining the proper personnel on these two committees.

A few suggestions on staffing these two committees is in order. Let us consider first the pulpit committee, because, all things considered, it is of primary significance.

Let us assume that there is a vacancy to fill on the pulpit committee. As you scan the list of possible nominees there is one overarching principle to keep in mind as you make your selection. It is this: Put on the pulpit committee only those persons who are unreservedly enthusiastic about you. It is desirable to have this committee made up of prominent, able, articulate, persuasive types. But all other considerations pale to insignificance before our above-stated first principle. When pondering a choice always ask the question "Will this person be as immovable as Gibraltar in resisting any suggestion that a change of pastors might be in order?" Unless the answer is an unqualified yes, if there is the faintest tinge of doubt about him in your mind, ruthlessly strike his name from the list. Only those pastors who have pulpit committees which are 100-per-cent, bottled-in-bond for them can expect consistently peaceful slumbers. All others frequently awaken in the middle of the night and toss restlessly through the small hours wondering what would happen in the event of a showdown.

Once you have established an effective pulpit committee you should turn your attention to strengthening the finance committee. A profile of the ideal member of the church finance committee would be: (1) A man whose annual income exceeds substantially the most optimistic estimate of what the church might pay its pastor in a period of unprecedented economic health. This is because it is unreasonable to expect anyone to vote the pastor more money than he makes himself. It puts too great a strain on human nature. Extensive research by the author has failed to uncover even one layman who puts a higher value on a clergy-

man's contribution to society than he puts on his own contribution. (2) A man whose income is derived largely from
salary. This is because capitalists, owners of businesses, and
coupon clippers think of salaries as "costs of business"—they
consider salaries as moneys they could retain if there were
any way of avoiding paying them. Thus, in this view,
salaried employees are necessary evils and the problem is to
calculate that salary figure at which—were it reduced further—the disgruntled employee would be an economic lia-
bility. Capitalists have an uncanny ability for estimating this
exact point. (3) A man whose personal contribution to the
church is minimal. (Nobody minds being generous with
other people's money.)

It is wise to exclude farmers, schoolteachers and women
from membership on the finance committee. Farmers are almost without exception on the stingy side. Schoolteachers
have no hope whatever of making any important money
and so will have little interest in seeing to it that you do.
And women are as emotional about money as they are about
everything else and thus highly unpredictable as to what
line they will take when salary-setting time rolls around.

Tell them they are in charge

We can sum up the correct philosophy of church administration by setting forth two general principles for you to
follow. If you let them shape your *modus operandi* success
is bound to follow. They are:

(1) Talk constantly about the democratic nature
of the church's organizational structure.[7]
(2) So organize your parish that all really important
decisions are made only by you.

[7.] Recommended phrases: "Democratic decisions democratically arrived
at"; "This is your church, and the people run it"; "The democratic
community of faith"; "Let us take counsel together"; "In the church
your vote counts as much as much as anyone's" (this is not strictly
true, of course, but it is a nice sentiment).

Do not try to operate on either one of these principles without the other. If you utilize only number two (as many impatient and headstrong pastors do try to operate, always with disastrous results), you will soon acquire a reputation as a dictator, as overbearing and unreasonable. Such a reputation never helps a pastor in getting on with the Lord's work. Also, if you make no attempt to conceal the fact that you really run things you will have no one else to blame when some plan or decision of yours backfires—as, sooner or later, it inevitably will.

If you attempt to operate on principle number one without including principle number two (as weak and indecisive pastors frequently do), you will exhaust your energies in the endless effort to persuade pigheaded parishioners to make decisions any seeing-eye dog of average intelligence could tell at a glance are the right decisions. You will spend your waking hours in a perpetual ensnarlment of red tape. You will be forever fighting to get off the lowest rung of the ecclesiastical ladder, a position which affords you an excellent view of your contemporaries as they race swiftly and joyously for the tantalizing prizes reachable only from the upper rungs. In short, you will spend your ministry trying to get a decision on what to do. You will never get anything done.

It is possible that among our readers there are especially sensitive souls who might consider the recommended *modus operandi* to be indistinguishable from plain chicanery. But it is far from that. Remember that our purpose is to lead our flocks to Beulah Land, and the quickest, easiest route to the blessed city is the right route.

Be assured that we have described that route. We know the way more surely than our dear Christian people else we would not deserve to be their shepherd. We would be unfaithful guides were we to let them thrash about in the wilderness when the land of milk and honey is just over the horizon. Yet, as benevolent pastors concerned for their spiritual welfare, we are aware that they need to think they are plotting the course. So it is out of our hearts of pastoral love that we arrange for them to believe they are guiding the pilgrimage. When, in the sweet by-and-by, they are able to understand this they will surely rise up and bless us for it.

CONDUCTING PUBLIC WORSHIP,

AN EXERCISE IN NOSTALGIA

V

Every seventh day for the remainder of your working life—minus, of course, the Sundays included in your annual vacation and those times when the infirmities of the flesh lay you low on the Lord's day—you will be conducting one or more services of public worship. In an average pastoral career you will perform this duty approximately four thousand times, not counting prayer meetings, community Thanksgiving services and short devotions for the Kiwanis Club and the Daughters of the American Revolution.

In the light of these statistics it requires no strenuous cerebration to conclude that here is a professional task in which a pastor should strive for competence. A pastor deficient in the skills necessary for the conducting of worship is analogous to a ship's captain who has failed to master navigation or a bank teller who can't count.

Cognizant of this, our seminaries devote no little time in teaching their future shepherds about worship. No doubt you have been put through the hoops of the theology of worship, the theory of hymn selection, the writing of prayers, the resource materials for building worship services, etc. You were taught to fashion the structure of the service after

the structure of the sixth chapter of Isaiah. You may even
have been instructed in the art of baptizing babies and the
intricacies of celebrating the Lord's Supper. These courses
fill out the curriculum nicely and appear to be highly
practical as described in the seminary catalogue. But they
will turn out to be of little use to you in your parish ministry.

The weakness of your seminary training in the art of worship is that it was built on the assumption that public worship is the public worship of God. No one, least of all the
author, would deny that this is a very nice assumption and
perhaps the way things ought to be. But in point of fact this
is not the way things are, and if you are so foolish as to
operate in the parish on this assumption not only will you
never be a bishop, you will never get out of the sticks.

What your good Christian people want to worship is not
God but themselves, although they do not know this and
only a pastor who expects to depart shortly for other fields
of endeavor will have the temerity to explain it to them.
But you need to know it, for this is the correct assumption
on which all successful public worship is built.

A moment's reflection on the facts will reinforce the
point. In this worldly, secular, materialistic age in which
the fast buck is king, in which it seems every man is out for
himself, in which—to our sorrow—the solid Christian virtues
of unselfish service and a willingness to sacrifice and sub-
ordinate vaunting personal ambition to the cause of the
kingdom are ignored, millions of people still go to church
Sunday after Sunday to do the same thing over and over.
They sing hymns, pray and listen to a choir and a preacher.

On the face of it, it is difficult to understand. Why do all
these people forsake warm beds and a leisurely perusal of
the Sunday paper to go and do what they did last Sunday
morning, and the Sunday before that, and the Sunday before that, and will be doing next Sunday morning, and the
Sunday after that, and the Sunday after that, etc.?

You may be certain that they do not make this extraordinary effort for the purpose of anything so abstract as

to worship God, however commendable such a motive would be. Leaving aside such contributory but not very important factors as force of habit and the need to flee from loneliness, the main force which pushes them out the door and brings them to the house of the Lord is the gratifying experience of worshiping themselves. The wise and loving pastor, then, will so perfect himself in the art of public worship that his spiritually hungry congregation will know that their worship needs will be provided for every Lord's Day at 11 A.M. (or thereabout). If you can manage this, your potential for rapid advancement is very high, and there is no theoretical reason why you cannot unless you have been snared in the net of the liturgical revival which goes in for form and ritual and all that. This revival is a movement of the ecclesiastical eggheads, and many young preachers are dazzled by it. But beware of it. Large congregations which pay high salaries have to keep business humming, and there aren't enough eggheads around to accomplish this.

The process of perfecting yourself in the art of worship leadership is really quite simple. A few easily comprehended principles strictly adhered to should suffice. First, you must purge yourself of all the worship theory with which the seminary infected you. This is because of the above-mentioned assumption that the preacher's task is to conduct the public worship of God. This is technically known as "objective worship," and in most parishes of the standard-brand churches there is no market for it.

What there is a market for is "subjective worship." This is the type of worship which has as its goal the creation of certain desired states of feeling in the worshiper. We usually refer to these states of feeling as "religious feelings" or "spiritual experiences." Such description is adequate for the layman. Indeed it is best that laymen generally don't delve any deeper into the psychology of worship than this. But for the professional clergyman these descriptions are too vague. He needs to know the component parts which, when put together, blend into a smoothly functioning mechanism that will do the job. It's like the average car owner, who is only slightly interested in what makes his car run so long as it runs properly. But the mechanic who looks after it must understand exactly what each gadget and gizmo contributes to the function of the vehicle.

How to produce the right feeling

What is the nature of the "religious feelings" we seek to create in our faithful churchgoers? You can read tons of books on the psychology of religious experience, from William James to an eminent modern psychologist-theologian who devotes frequent space in his syndicated daily newspaper column to counsel on how to pep up church services. We clerics ought to be filled with gratitude that this noted layman and authority on public worship generously uses his national platform to popularize these sane and sensible views. He understands, even if many clergymen do not, that the kind of worship service which manufactures in the congregation the feelings it wants to feel is one of the most effective methods of filling the house and keeping the customers coming back Sunday after Sunday. A veteran churchgoer, he is also a student of homiletics (sermon preparation). His frequent advice in his column on how to be a live wire in the pulpit should be required reading for all clergymen. He is indeed a man richly endowed with talent.

However much you study the subject, though, you will eventually discover that what we have referred to as "religious feelings" may be composed of many elements, but by far the largest single ingredient is the emotion which is called "nostalgia." As a matter of fact, there is no scientific evidence to contradict the contention that religious feelings and the emotion of nostalgia are one and the same thing.

It is a valid working rule that most people, as they grow older, find life increasingly complex, their responsibilities weighing heavier and heavier, the years passing at an ever swifter pace. This produces in them a longing for what they imagine, in retrospect, was a far simpler and happier period of their lives than in all probability it actually was. Freudian psychologists would consider this phenomenon a mild form of the subconscious desire to return to a prior condition of perfect security and contentment—that is, to return to the womb. As Shelley Berman has said, "Let's face it—we all want to go back."

But no matter. The significant item is that they believe it was happier. This is all you need for your working hypothesis.

So the ordering and execution of a public worship service is, at its best, an exercise in nostalgia. If you can consistently inject into the order of worship those items which will trigger a nostalgic response in your congregation (and you can), you have a running start and momentum with which to climb the hill of clerical preferment, all the spiritual and material goodies reserved for popular and successful servants of the Lord are coming nearer to your grasp; you will soon be a commissioned officer in the church militant.

If you study the truly successful evangelists you will note that they all use music—congregational singing, anthems, solos—to manipulate the audience's feelings and enchant the paying customers. What would Billy Sunday have been without Homer Rodeheaver? The lesson here is that music is the number one weapon in the preacher's arsenal. The devil fears one good, old-fashioned hymn sung with bite and zowie by an enthusiastic congregation more than he fears ten thousand sermons denouncing the sinful pastimes of the world and the flesh.

Nothing evokes feelings of nostalgia in faithful Christian churchgoers like a hymn they learned in Sunday School, or sang frequently in the dear little church of their childhood surrounded by family and friends blasting away with them. It dredges up memories of carefree times, Sunday dinners, church picnics, the early exciting stirrings of sex impulses so mysterious and so wicked, and an avalanche of other reveries all mixed together into an emotional omelet which is incredibly tasty to the spirit and providing rich nourishment for the soul. This is what we mean by nostalgia.

The good and the bad hymns

The competent cleric, then, will take pains to familiarize himself with the hymnal which is used by the Sunday congregation. Usually it will be the official hymnal of his particular denomination, and these are pretty much the same. Hymn book committees are generally composed of trained musicians with esoteric tastes, and practical pastors who know what people want and need, so the result is a hymnal with two types of sacred songs—good and bad.

You will lighten your labors for the years to come and prevent the inclusion of unsuitable hymns when, as will frequently be the case, you are forced by the exigencies of your multitudinous duties to give the preparation of Sunday's service a lick and a promise, if you will set aside a half-day now to go through your personal copy of the hymnal and mark each hymn contained therein "good" or "bad." It would, however, be wise to do this marking in code. Your hymnal might fall into the hands of some musically literate member of your congregation whose judgment would differ from yours, and who might take offense at your classifications were they plainly readable. In any event, code markings of anything denote professionalism and smack of inside information. Then, if you will list all the page numbers of those hymns which you have classified "good" on the flyleaf, all you need do for the remainder of your professional career of putting together worship services is to select the hymns from this list of numbers. When the pressure of time is especially heavy you need not even ponder which of these "good" hymns to use. Simply pick three or four numbers at random from the list on the flyleaf. You can't possibly go wrong.

And what is the basis or principle by which this division

is accomplished? Remember what we are seeking in those songs with high nostalgia-evoking potential. The simplest method of ferreting out these hymns is to classify the contents of the book as to whether a hymn is "objective" or "subjective." Then discard all hymns marked "objective" and use only those on the subjective list.

And the rule for testing a hymn is this: If it emphasizes the attributes of God—His majesty, power, mercy, goodness, love, etc.—or recounts in some manner the story of Jesus, it is an objective hymn and thus, with possible rare exceptions, unsuitable for a public worship service. If on the other hand, the hymn is preoccupied with the feelings, reactions, desires, hopes and longings of the individual worshiper it is subjective and guaranteed to have a religious kick in it.

Illustrations are always more helpful than general rules, so let us consider examples of good and bad hymns.

Some strikes against "A Mighty Fortress"

One hymn which is sung with great frequency in many churches is Luther's "A Mighty Fortress." It is high on the sacred hit parade among seminarians, theologians and the musically educated. This fact alone is enough to make the parish pastor question its acceptability in his congregation, but there are other sound and cogent reasons why it is a bad hymn.

Notice the text. It says:

> A Mighty Fortress is Our God,
> A bulwark never failing;
> Our helper He, amid the flood
> Of mortal ills prevailing:

or this:

> Did we in our own strength confide,
> Our striving would be losing;
> Were not the right man on our side,
> The man of God's own choosing:

The hymn has four stanzas, all in this same lugubrious vein, stressing the power and greatness of God in contrast with the miserable helplessness of man left to his own devices. This is an objective hymn. Its weaknesses are as follows:

(1) It gives all the attention and praise to God and none to the worshiper. It talks incessantly about the Almighty and His battle with the powers of darkness—a theological concept remote from the thinking and experience of the good Christian souls under our pastoral care, and too vague for them to grasp or to interest them. It speaks in very uncomplimentary terms of man, and not many people get any spiritual uplift from being told they are miserable and ineffective creatures.

(2) It lacks any warm, human, comforting, inspiring sentiment. In one stanza, for example, it advises us to "Let goods and kindred go, this mortal life also." You could scan a thousand congregations with radar and go through them with a Geiger counter without detecting even one Christian who is even faintly inclined to follow such advice.

(3) "A Mighty Fortress" is not sung in any but Lutheran Sunday Schools, and was not in the repertoire of the small rural and town churches in which most of your congregation was raised. Therefore, it has no connection with any previous pleasant experience of theirs. Therefore it has a nostalgia-evoking rating of absolute zero.

(4) The music to which it is set (*"Ein' Feste Burg"*— also by Martin Luther) is not a good tune. It has no lilt or bounce to it, no blood-quickening rhythm, no soul-soothing strains which linger in the heart. It is, for your purposes— and in spite of the high esteem in which it has been held by musical and theological highbrows for over four hundred years—a bad hymn.

The assurances of "Blessed Assurance"

Now let us look at an example of a good hymn. For our illustration we have selected Fanny J. Crosby's great and famous gospel song, "Blessed Assurance."[1] Note the elements of strength in this hymn.

(1) It focuses on the internal, spiritual experiences of the individual worshiper. Here are parts of the text:

"Blessed assurance" (this means *my* blessed assurance) "Jesus is *mine*"; "Perfect submission" (*my* perfect submission); "perfect delight" (*I* am perfectly delighted); "Visions of rapture" (this means *I* am filled with spiritual thrills) "now burst on my sight . . ."; "*I* in my saviour am happy and blest"; "Filled with His goodness" (*I* am filled with his goodness) "lost in His love" (*I* am completely abandoned in this love experience). Then the song has what so many hymns lack—a refrain to be sung after each stanza. "This is *my* story, this is *my* song, Praising *my* saviour all the day long."

(2) The music to which it is set ("Assurance") is a splendid sentimental tune, easily remembered even by a backward member of the Jukes family after one hearing. It has a syrupy quality about it, with the added advantage that it lends itself to loud and raucous congregational singing—a combination which is difficult to come by in a hymn and hard to beat for the purposes of public worship. Belted out by a churchful of enthusiastic Christians, with everyone unleashing a few extra decibels on the refrain, it will lift even the most stolid clod in the congregation out of his grubby, materialistic, unimaginative, uninspiring everyday concerns and transport him to Elysian fields of spiritual bliss.

(3) Everyone in your faithful flock except the very young sang this good old song of salvation every week in Sunday School, and not infrequently sang it again an hour later in the church service. It opens a floodgate releasing a lakeful of dammed up memories which pour over the worshiper in a blessed cascade of nostalgia. So, through this one little song

[1.] We could have selected any Fanny J. Crosby hymn. She was one of the truly inspired sacred hymnodists of her age.

he has had a good, true, warm, authentic, inspiring religious experience, an experience the like of which he cannot obtain much of anywhere but in the church. You can readily perceive that, as a device for building congregational loyalty, consistently high church attendance, and a willingness to shell out generous amounts of hard cash for the Lord's work (and for the Lord's diligent and faithful servant who is the pastoral incumbent, and who has been wise enough and competent enough to provide him with this priceless experience), it has few equals. This is a subjective hymn. This is a GOOD hymn.

It has been said that, had Miss Crosby through some misguided impulse have gotten married, she would never have written this and other inspiring hymns. How grateful we are that she sublimated her normal human inclinations, which were then able to burst through into matchless religious poetry. Her case illustrates, beyond doubt, the validity of the celibate life for certain religious vocations.

The greatest hymn ever written

Perhaps the greatest hymn ever written, judged not by the limited and unrealistic standards of professional church musicians but by the tests of usefulness, popularity and effectiveness in our battle to promote and encourage the Christian life at the level of the parish ministry, is C. Austin Miles' masterpiece "In the Garden."

Since it is almost a perfect model of what you are looking for in the hymns you select for public worship we quote the entire text.

Stanza 1

> *I* come to the garden alone,
> While the dew is still on the roses,
> And the Voice *I* hear
> Falling on *my* ear
> The Son of God discloses.

Refrain

> And He walks with *me,*
> And He talks with *me,*
> And He tells *me I* am His own;
> And the joy *we* share
> As *we* tarry there,
> None other has ever known.

Stanza 2

> He speaks, and the sound of His Voice
> Is so sweet the birds Hush their singing,
> And the melody
> That He gives to *me*
> Within *my* heart is ringing.

Refrain

Stanza 3

> I'd stay in the garden with Him,
> Though the night around *me* be falling,
> But He bids *me* go;
> Through the voice of woe
> His voice to *me* is calling.

Refrain

You will notice that the personal pronouns are italicized. When the hymn is sung through with refrain after each stanza the personal pronoun is used twenty-seven times. This is a measure of the surpassing skill of the writer and tells us that he was a man not only of extraordinary spiritual sensitivity and insight, but knowledgeable in the tastes and religious needs of the kind of good Christian people you will be serving.

For one thing, he never lets their attention stray from themselves, which is the subject, he knows, in which they are most vitally interested. In the second place, he throws the switch activating the nostalgia mechanism in the first five words, "I come to the Garden . . ." Everybody has had a garden, or has been in a garden. "Garden" is a word

associated with beauty, pleasure, peace, retreat from the
world, man's original innocence before it was spoiled by
sin,[2] etc. Then the hymn writer nails down this idyllic
memory picture with the line "While the dew is still on the
roses . . ." A lovely rose dampened by pure atmospheric
moisture (who thinks of atomic fallout or belching chimneys
befouling God's good clean air at a time like this?) is a
symbol—to the average man scratching out a living five days
a week at a job he despises, surrounded and saturated with
the ugly, the dirty, the unlovely things of life—of created
perfection, of complete separation from this sordid, wicked
world, of bliss beyond any happiness his earth-bound human imaginings are capable of encompassing. Indubitably,
these few words alone are enough to do the job we want
done. Limitations of space do not permit us to analyze it
further, but use the hymn often, about every other Sunday
or so.

It will strike you as you pore over your hymnal, that the
preferred subjective-type numbers in most cases have texts
which are little short of gibberish. What does it mean, for
example, when that grand old favorite of the years, "Sweet
Hour of Prayer," has us sing,

> Till, from Mt. Pisgah's lofty height,
> I view my home, and take my flight:
> This robe of flesh I'll drop, and rise
> To seize the everlasting prize,
> And shout, while passing through the air,
> Farewell, Farewell, sweet hour of prayer?

If you didn't know this is part of a hymn which has comforted countless Christian souls, you might take it for a
message in a code which defies all efforts to break it. Nor
can you escape the conclusion, as you segregate the good

2. A lot of sinning probably goes on in gardens, beginning with Adam
and Eve down to the present. But people, somehow, just don't associate the two ideas.

hymns from the bad ones, that very few modern, prosperous, comfortable and contented Christians can sing these precious old religious ballads and mean a word of what they are saying.

Picture, if you will, the successful, hard-nosed executives in your congregation arriving at the church in their Cadillacs and Lincolns dressed in Society Brand suits with their wives in mink stoles joining in,

> Others may choose this vain world if they will,
> I will follow Jesus;
> All else forsaking, will cleave to him still,
> I will follow Him

or imagine the president of the local bank chanting,

> Take my silver and my gold,
> Not a mite would I withhold . . .

or a wealthy bachelor with a stable of comely lady friends and a taste for exotic foods and rare wines solemnly intoning,

> Earthly pleasures vainly call me . . .
> Nothing worldly shall enthrall me . . .

or the average collection of Christian saints who know full well that the church is split into denominational segments too numerous to count pooling their enthusiastic voices in,

> We are not divided, all one body we,
> One in hope and doctrine, one in charity.

Whenever someone takes a poll to determine the most popular hymn of all, it invariably turns out to be "The Old Rugged Cross." On the whole, it has probably generated more religious sentiment, more holy horsepower in more people than any other sacred music. Yet it has four stanzas, plus refrain, which affirm that above all else I love that old rugged cross, nothing else has nearly so much attraction for me, so I'll cherish it as my dearest possession, a state-

ment which practically nobody in your flock can make and
be even in the general vicinity of the truth. But Sunday
after Sunday they make it. And when asked to name their
favorite hymn reply without hesitation "The Old Rugged
Cross."

Here is a mystery. How can relatively sane, intelligent
people happily sing what amounts to nonsense, or claim,
through song, to believe what they obviously do not believe,
or promise via hymnody to do what they haven't the faintest
inclination to do, and would be stunned if, after the amen,
were told to go and do what they just finished saying they
were going to do ("Take my silver and my gold, Not a mite
would I withhold" for example). As you ponder this
paradox your confidence in the author's counsel may be
weakened.

But we urge you to respect our long experience in these
matters. And the explanation of the phenomenon is obvious.
It is that people hardly ever pay any attention to the words
when they sing hymns. It is as if they know, in advance,
that the words don't mean anything anyway. If they like
the tune, if it is associated with pleasant experiences, if the
music falls agreeably on their ears they make no demands
on the text of rationality or poetic quality or anything else.

Though the late H. L. Mencken claimed no one ever went
broke underestimating the taste of the American public,
there is a level of taste and quality (quite low, to be sure)
below which you should not descend when you classify a
hymn as good. The author advises against the use of such
numbers as "Life Is Like a Mountain Railroad," "That Old-
Time Religion" and "There Ain't No Flies on Jesus," no
matter how soul-stirring they may be. Also, as you make
your way upward in the grade of churches you pastor, you
should remember to throw in one bad (objective) hymn
each Sunday as a sop to the minority of culture vultures in
the congregation. This protects you against any possible
accusation that you are a man of low tastes and insensitive
ear.

Soft music and the prayer tone

Next, you will be well advised to exert careful control over the non-congregational musical portions of the service— anthems, organ voluntaries, etc.

Insist that your choirmaster use only those anthems with catchy or sentimental tunes on the order of "My God and I" (which is one of the half-dozen greatest choir numbers ever composed and is the anthem equivalent of "In The Garden"). Always remember that you have to keep a sharp eye on choirmasters or they will be trotting out Bach chorales or dissonant modern stuff, types of music totally unsuitable for the purposes of public worship. Pacify them by letting them use this kind of music in an occasional choir recital.

Organ music should avoid the strong and the loud. For preludes such numbers as "Claire de Lune" and "Ave Maria" induce a near-hypnotic state in worshipers, which is what we are striving for. People under hypnosis, as you know, are easy to manipulate. Therefore, always have the organist play very softly during the pastoral prayer, and during other parts of the service when congregational attention is not required.

There is little else to say about conducting public worship after instruction on the choice and use of music, for if music is used correctly it doesn't matter much what else you do.

One always reads from the Holy Scriptures, of course, and most congregations would sense that something was missing if you omitted it, though they might not immediately realize what. But the Bible is an obscure and hidden book for modern Christians, so it is best not to overdo its use. One way to make the reading of the Scriptures meaningful is to memorize a passage each week and recite it with the lectern Bible closed (to emphasize the fact that you are reciting). This will electrify the congregation and promote laudatory talk in the parish. It calls for only a small effort on your part, but your people will think it great. As long as we have to read Scripture in the service one might as well get some mileage out of it.

For public prayer remember never to lapse into a normal conversational voice. Listen carefully to the pastoral praying of successful veterans of the cross. Without exception they have developed a "prayer tone" which has a rich, resonant "religious" quality about it. When they say solemnly "Let us pray" you can almost hear the shifting of their vocal gears as they prepare to speak to the Almighty. You won't be able to come by this "prayer tone" at once. It takes years of practice, and many a clergyman claims that, as he comes to retirement, he is just hitting his stride in the use of his voice for public prayer. But work hard on it, for few large churches will tolerate a pastor who gives an undistinguished performance in the pastoral prayer.

When baptizing babies always dip a rose in the font and shake it gently over the infant's fuzzy little cranium. Then present the rose to the mother (do this with a bit of a flourish). Soon this baptismal rite will become an exceedingly popular item in your service and people will look forward with anticipation to those Sundays when it is to be observed.

Managing the successful wedding ceremony

You will want to perfect yourself, too, in the conducting of wedding ceremonies. If you can get for yourself a reputation for putting on a dandy wedding it will raise you in the esteem of the community and add considerably to your income. Every community has a significant proportion of its population made up of people who never go near a church except in times of dire need, such as when they want to get married. Since it makes no difference whatever to them what church they use they gravitate to the one whose pastor is known to put on the best nuptial show. There is no reason why this should not be you.

A formal wedding, like Gaul, is divided into three parts. First comes the initial arrangements, including a counseling session with the supposedly happy couple. Next is the rehearsal, and finally the ceremony itself.

There is a trend today among younger clergymen to spend several lengthy sessions with a prospective bride and groom counseling them on everything under the sun. This takes an enormous amount of time and is not at all necessary. About all you need do in the initial session is to establish the hour of the wedding and the rehearsal, and be certain the music is arranged for. The average wedding fee, you will discover, hardly warrants wasting excessive amounts of time on this section of your pastoral duty.

The rehearsal is apt to be a trial. First, everybody is usually late. Experienced pastors know it is impossible to start a rehearsal at the appointed hour and so never hurry to be on time themselves. Then, the bride's mother frequently shows up with a copy of Emily Post under her arm and a managerial expression on her face. She will make all sorts of outlandish and impractical suggestions, directions and demands. You will have to suffer her as best you can and manage to sidetrack her more ridiculous ideas of how the wedding should be run off.

Also, grooms have a habit of anesthetizing themselves against the trauma of their loss of freedom with several large belts from the bottle prior to the rehearsal and will comprehend only dimly, if at all, any directions you give him. Another potential area of trouble is the music, particularly the solos. Brides have a tendency to be adamant about their choice of music and it will often call for all your persuasiveness to dissuade them from their tasteless and ill-considered selections. In general, encourage a bride to stick to the time-tested secular pieces such as "O Promise Me" and "I Love You Truly." Spiritual-type girls often want some sacred music sung at their weddings, but discourage this if you can. People expect to hear the familiar tunes they associate with weddings when they go to a wedding, and if they don't they feel that the ceremony hasn't been quite up to snuff, and will think that you aren't capable of putting on a first-rate production.

Then, too, the thoughtless selection of sacred music for a wedding can contribute to a connubial catastrophe. Two pertinent examples of inexperienced clergymen muffing the ball through their failure to scrutinize carefully the bride's selections of solos should suffice to emphasize the importance of this pastoral responsibility. In one case, the bride, a young lady of amazonian proportions was marrying a meek lad so diminutive in stature as to make the contrast between them a subject of community comment. Unfortunately, the bride insisted on the use of her two favorite hymns which were 'For the Love of God" and "I'd Rather Have Jesus." In the other instance the ceremony ended with the congregation singing "We Shall See Them Coming, Numberless as the Sands of the Sea." How much better it would have been had these girls chosen something tasteful and appropriate such as "The Sweetheart of Sigma Chi" or "Will You Love Me in September as You Did in May?"

One so-called sacred number you can recommend without fear is Malot's setting of "The Lord's Prayer," which is really more in the realm of popular music than of sacred music. It is well to use it as a part of the ceremony itself. As the bride and groom kneel together with the soloist pouring forth the sweet strains of this music you create a sentimental picture which will bring tears of joy to the eyes of the assembled guests. This enhances your reputation as a marrying parson and should generate a lot of new business.

There is nothing to the ceremony itself if you have had a proper rehearsal. Just don't forget to show up. And get to the church early enough to calm and comfort the groom. Don't worry about the bride. She has been pointing for this moment since she was a little girl and she doesn't intend to blow it now. Nervous brides are a rarity. They generally have about them the look of a warrior who has vanquished every foe and is about to receive the laurel wreath.

A final word on conducting worship. Remember that it matters little what you do as you lead, but it matters a great deal how you do it. Avoid displays of excessive vitality or enthusiasm in voice or manner, except in the sermon, where it is permissible to pound the pulpit now and then for emphasis and to awaken slumbering worshipers. We shouldn't be pompous, but on the other hand we shouldn't be far from it. A solemn demeanor and a "holy tone" will send your faithful people on their way to their roast beef and funny papers with a truly religious feeling and a genuine sense of having been to church.

VI

A medical doctor can slice and/or dose his patients and be done with them, except for collecting the bill. A lawyer can draw a will or sue. A teacher can bore his classes three or four hours a day and spend his evenings with a pipe and a detective story. We live in the time of the specialist. The daily routine of most business and professional men is more or less the same. Their activities are related to a field of endeavor which they have mastered because nearly anyone can master a certain task if he performs it often enough and is not distracted by duties of a different nature and calling for another set of skills.

Not so the preacher. He is supposed to be an orator, administrator, business manager, psychologist, school superintendent, scholar, community leader, fund raiser, teacher, after-dinner speaker and master of ceremonies, to name a few of the trades in which he needs some degree of proficiency.

No one, of course, is going to shine at all these things. And it is not necessary that you should. Recent research has shown us that 93.786 per cent of those men who do become bishops are not especially good at any single pastoral skill but are passably capable in all of them. What you need to do, as you prepare yourself in the early days of your career for eventual membership in the select circle of the ecclesiastical elite, is to learn how to discharge the miscellaneous duties of the ministry so that you will be recognized as competent but without letting them consume any considerable portion of your time or energy.

Among those duties which you will be expected to perform satisfactorily is a group which are of a minor nature but each of which some of your good people think is your major task.

How to live with the Sunday School

Every church, as you know, has attached to it a number of subsidiary organizations. Most important of these is the Sunday School. While the church has been going now for some two thousand years the Sunday School has been around only about two hundred years. Amazingly, in those two hundred years it has nearly caught up with the church in size, organizational loyalty, and the reverence with which its zealots treat it. It is, in fact, a separate religious institution masquerading as a part of your church but actually in direct competition with the church. It has its own organizational structure, its own budget, its own promotional program, its own worship services. Therefore many of its adherents consider it an adequate substitute for the church, as witness the big procession heading for home as soon as Sunday School is dismissed. These people never think of attending church. They get their weekly dose of religion in Sunday School.

You may be distressed at this state of affairs in your early pastorates, but the wisest course for you to follow is to learn to live with it, because the situation will not change. Remember that you are responsible for the Sunday School. You will have to work with it. So we include two principles to keep in mind at all times as you deal with it, which—if you observe them scrupulously—should enable you to stay out of trouble.

The first principle is that the Sunday School is a sacred cow, and thus should never be criticized, improved or tampered with in any way. The fury of a woman scorned is a mild irritation compared with the animosity elicited from a good and faithful Sunday School superintendent to whom it is suggested that the S.S. could stand a little refurbishing. If you, his pastor, are so witless as to suggest it you will succeed only in mobilizing the entire Sunday School organization to a dedicated and unrelenting effort to oust you from the church.

So, whatever your private opinion, let your public utterances as to the S.S. be excessively laudatory. Lay it on thick. It is like complimenting a woman—never be afraid that you are overdoing it, because you can't.

The second principle is that you must not confuse the function of the Sunday School with education. Admittedly the name "school" is misleading, and inexperienced pastors nearly always waste enormous amounts of time and effort trying to make of the S.S. a teaching enterprise before they discover that the Sunday School does not exist in order that the pupils may learn anything. In fact, the genuinely superior Sunday Schools are those which impart the least factual information to their students. This apparent paradox is explained when you remember that S.S. teachers are volunteers, that they are dealing with material they know nothing about (and probably haven't even read), so whatever they do manage to teach is likely to be misinformation—which is worse than no information.

What the S.S. does exist for is:

(1) A baby-sitting service.

Harassed young parents, badly in need of sleep or time for other activities impracticable with small children all over the place, look on the S.S. as the perfect, or nearly perfect, solution to their Sunday morning problem. It is entirely free (except for pennies for the collection), and enlightened churches have what is known as "extended sessions" in their Sunday Schools which keep the kids for upwards of three hours. Little wonder that the S.S. is highly thought of by the young families of the community.

(2) A form of entertainment for adults who get up early on Sunday morning and don't care to read the Sunday paper or watch TV. And what else is there for older people to do at 9 A.M. on Sunday morning?

Most churches have one to four large, enthusiastic and loyal adult Sunday School classes. Sometimes they are built around the personality of a teacher. In such instances the teacher is a direct competitor of the preacher and nothing delights him so much as outdrawing the preacher on Sunday morning, a not infrequent situation.

Other adult classes prosper by appealing to a certain age group. The so-called young married class is an example of this species. It usually has a clever and distinctive name such as "Cum Duble," "Twosies" or "Ball-and-Chain," and goes in heavily for social events.

You will be expected to visit these classes, and the average freshly minted seminary graduate is appalled at the theology dispensed in them. It ranges from fundamentalist pietism through salvation by thinking gorgeous thoughts, with both extremes frequently included in the same lesson by the same teacher, with no one bothered in the least by the inconsistencies.

Take your cue from the class and don't be bothered either. You simply can't afford to be finicky about theology when dealing with the S.S. The surest way to kill off a large, popular adult Sunday School class is to insist that it devote itself to serious study. Americans have, for a long time now, been told that if a group of people who know nothing whatever about a subject spend an hour or so pooling their ignorant and uninformed opinions the end product will be insights whose truth is beyond question and an occult wisdom unobtainable by lesser methods. This is the faith on which the adult S.S. class is founded, and to destroy it is to destroy the institution.

Remember, too, that the religious education enterprise of your denomination is a powerful vested interest. Your publishing house sells S.S. lesson materials by the bale, a vastly profitable undertaking. Also, there is a strongly entrenched religious education hierarchy with hundreds of employees which is dedicated to keeping the S.S. movement large and vigorous. You are in no position to fight a battle with this well-equipped army, so don't try. Accept the Sunday School as a fact of your professional life, pat it on the back as often as possible, and refrain from any attempt to change it.

Hitting it off with the ladies

Like unto the Sunday School is the Women's Society or Ladies' Aid or whatever your denomination calls its female auxiliary organization. It, too, has aspects of a separate denomination—a local president and an astonishingly large slate of officers, a separate and complete religious program including worship services, mission projects, budget, etc., and an aggressive national hierarchical structure. It also has many members who find in it a sufficient source for their religious needs and who therefore have little or nothing to do with the church.

If you think the author issued a strong warning against tampering with the Sunday School, then double it and raise it to the tenth power when dealing with the ladies. If there is any one rule the breaking of which you cannot survive, it is "Never, never, interfere in any way with the operation of the female auxiliary of your Church." These good faithful Marthas will try your patience with the incredible dullness of their programs, the unpredictability of their administrative decisions,[1] and their taste in wallpaper, paint, etc., which—in your early and smaller churches—they express

---

[1.] Women make all decisions by some superrational, mystical, intuitive process totally incomprehensible to men.

by decorating the parsonage. But they do raise whopping amounts of hard cash, a portion of which finds it way into the operating budget of the church and thus helps underwrite your salary. So to offend the ladies in any way is to work against your own best interests.

The author has little counsel to offer in the matter of getting along with the Ladies' Aid. Some clergymen distinguish themselves in this pastoral activity, some don't. But an analysis of fifty-three preachers who have had signal success in dealing with female auxiliaries, even though the latest research methods were employed (including feeding statistical data into the maw of an electronic computer) has failed to isolate any clear-cut method of approach guaranteed to work. In the light of these confusing results the author can only conclude that some charismatic quality as yet undetectable by IBM is probably what gets the job done.

Some pastors with outstanding records in hitting it off with the ladies claim that charm is the answer—which you either have or you don't have. Others rely heavily on prayer. In any case, the author intends to pursue this line of research and upon uncovering significant information will publish it immediately—perhaps in later editions of this book.

The art of pastoral counseling

Let us now consider the art of pastoral counseling. We refer to it as an art because that is what it is in spite of our seminaries' efforts to make of it a science.

Pastoral counseling is very much the vogue these days. It has achieved status by becoming a separate, specialized academic discipline with its own department in graduate schools of theology, and its own professional journals, and a fast-growing nomenclature understood only by its initiates. Some seminarians—a growing proportion of each graduating class in fact—frantically search for jobs as hospital chaplains or ministers of counseling or faculty positions where counseling is taught in order to devote all their time to this field, free from the interruptions and annoyances of parish work.

Probably you have come to your first pastorate with the ambition of becoming, as rapidly as possible, a wise, benevolent and beloved spiritual counselor to your flock and the community in general. What will happen is that you will sit for weeks and months in your empty study vainly hoping for someone to get their personal life into such a mess that they will come to you to straighten it out for them. As the passing days deny this hope you may in despair conclude that you have been assigned to the one sinless parish in all Christendom.

Your parish is, of course, as well furnished with wrong-doers as any other. But even those who might be inclined to seek pastoral counsel are put off by your unlined face and hair as yet untinged by gray. People assume that preachers of any age are unacquainted with the less savory aspects of human behavior and are easily shocked by con-fession of any species of sin more spectacular than an occasional errant thought. But a young preacher is thought to be so naïve that he would be entirely useless in extricating a bona fide sinner from the consequences of his escapades. So it is not the uniquely high rate of virtue in your parish which is preventing you from becoming a counselor to the guilt-ridden, but your youth.

When the day does come that a parishioner makes an appointment to "talk over a personal problem" you must quell your excitement. You will be anticipating a techni-color tale of lurid misdoings, but what you will get is a long and tedious account of a petty personal peeve from someone who has exhausted his (or more likely her) list of captive listeners and has turned to you as a last resort.

But don't be crushed. By the time you have put in twenty years on the job you will have heard, in clinical detail, descriptions of every possible form of human misconduct. You will discover that original sin is quite unoriginal in its specific expressions. This fact is the cause of great boredom among experienced pastors, psychiatrists and other personal counselors. What will shock the pants off you the first few times you hear it will eventually become dull with repetition. The time will come, although you cannot possibly believe it now as you wait for a counseling case to come to your lonely study, when you will be able—after hearing a sentence or two from your counselee—to finish the story for them in every particular except names and dates. When the author of the Book of Ecclesiastes wrote that there is nothing new under the sun he was undoubtedly speaking out of long experience as a pastoral counselor; after all, he is still referred to as "the preacher." Contrary to popular belief, a veteran pastor is the least shockable man in the community, with the possible exception of a newspaper reporter on the police beat.

The experts tell us that effective personal counseling takes a sinful amount of time. And time for this sort of thing is something you don't have. You need to employ your working hours in raising money, attending meetings and making contacts which will help you up the hill of a successful career in the church. Time spent in counseling is time lost to the main and central concerns of our calling. However, if you will keep in mind two or three techniques as you seek to become a proficient pastoral counselor without wasting undue amounts of time you will get by in good shape.

The first is to convince yourself that no special skill is needed for this area of your work. Every now and then you may be tempted to attend the many clinical training sessions for pastors which have become so popular in recent years. But this is not at all necessary. Mainly, what you need to do in counseling situations is to listen. Most people love to talk about themselves. They especially enjoy talking about their sins, and tend to exaggerate their wickedness. But very few people, they discover, are willing to listen to them for anything like a satisfying length of time. They have, then, two alternatives: they can seek out a psychiatrist who will listen at a set rate of twenty to fifty dollars an hour; or they can go to the pastor who will do the same thing for nothing.

No one doubts that listening to a counselee spill the beans is—for him—excellent therapy. But he is likely to spill them a lot faster to the psychiatrist at those rates than he is to the pastor who, after all, is costing him nothing.

You must restrain yourself from actually giving your counselees any counsel. In the first place, this isn't what they want from you so it is unnecessary. In the second place, they might actually follow your advice and then—if it turned out badly—hate you for it.

Just listen. And when you decide you have listened long enough have a word of prayer with the counselee, rise from your chair, look at your watch, and bid them good day. And that's all there is to pastoral counseling.

One or two other unavoidable obligations of our sacred profession deserve a passing observation.

Many churches now have men's organizations. Unlike the female auxiliary these are no trouble at all. They are simply a slightly sanctified version of the Kiwanis Club. See to it that at their monthly dinner meetings the fellows are well-fed and well-entertained. That is all they want or need.

When you advance to the grade of parish which maintains an office in the church, surround yourself with the accouterments of executive efficiency. Among these are wall-to-wall carpeting, a large desk, luxurious furniture, a dictating machine, and a push-button telephone. This has the effect of impressing the people, strengthening your image as a successful pastor-executive, and sustaining your own ego.

Finally, promote yourself a month's vacation as soon as you are able. The author lists this under the heading of "unavoidable obligations" because it is an essential status symbol for the clergyman on his way up. You may have only enough money to get out of town and be forced to spend a miserable double fortnight free-loading off your inlaws, but do it. Preachers with only two weeks off when they are in their third pastorate probably will spend their professional life in churches which grant a two-week vacation. If you can't manage a month off, no one will believe you can manage anything else and will let you languish in the foothills of the mountain named ecclesiastical success.

To help you remember that these unavoidable obligations, though minor in nature, must be mastered, we close with the words St. Paul appended to a somewhat similar list of offices when instructing a young pastor: "Practice these duties, devote yourself to them," he wrote, "so that all may see your progress."

GETTING INTO THE MAJOR LEAGUES

VII

We will assume that you, an eager, ambitious and diligent young preacher who is wholly dedicated to serving the Lord in the highest possible echelons of the church militant (for the truly dedicated holy man desires above all other things to render maximum service through his blessed calling), have soaked up the wisdom in these pages and are laboring mightily to polish and perfect yourself along the lines herein described. It occurs to the author that you might assume this is all you need do to cinch a bishop's throne, that your progress toward the grand prize of our high calling will be automatic, that the rapidity with which you overtake the purple will be governed only by your speed in assimilating and applying to your work the skills recommended in this text.

It is incumbent upon the author to warn you that such is not the case, that to depend on professional competence alone is to rest your future career on a frail reed. Hundreds of intelligent, capable and well-trained clergyman have naïvely trusted in their ability to get them ahead and are perplexed and discouraged to find themselves at middle age enduring the privation and boredom of village parishes, surrounded by cornfields and loutish parishioners and not much else.

Now this in no sense invalidates the instruction in previous chapters of this book. You *must* master the skills in which we have been tutoring you. But you must also do something more. You must learn how to pick your way through the obstacles distributed on the trail like a mine field by those who have made it to the top of the ecclesiastical mountain. These obstacles are designed by those who have arrived to slow down the eager young clerics panting up the glory road behind them. While this may seem callous and cruel and un-Christian to tenderfoot divines, you will understand someday that this is the church's way of eliminating the unworthy, the defective, the flawed seekers after spiritual power. It is, to be sure, an application to the spiritual realm of Darwin's principle of the survival of the fittest. And if an occasional injustice is done, if, now and then, an able but unwary pilgrim is waylaid on the journey to the celestial city—or, on the other hand, some boob picks his way through by sheer luck—it is a little price to pay to insure the church a small but steady procession of leaders who have made it across the stormy Jordan. But for you the rigors of the trip to the top can be reduced substantially by a thorough briefing on the terrain ahead. This is what we now propose to do for you.

The first requirement of any successful campaign or plan of attack is to eliminate, insofar as is possible, the element of chance. This is best accomplished by carefully plotting the entire operation and then executing the plan step by step.

Since you are freshly ordained and standing on the bottom rung of the ministerial ladder you are probably twenty-six or twenty-seven years of age and the proud but nervous possessor of an insignificant pastorate in some God-forsaken town several miles from nowhere. You are a rookie in the Lord's game, and you have been assigned—as are most rookies—to a Class D league. But you are filled with the giddy sense of being a certified professional.

Your first inclination will be to entertain visions of a spectacular performance out here in the bushes. You will dream of this down-at-the-heels parish suddenly coming to life, of the natives emerging from their spiritual torpor under your inspired preaching to renovate the church, forsake their ungodly ways, and unite behind you to transform the community into a model of decency and Christian behavior.

This, of course, will not happen. Such congregations as are assigned to beginning preachers have seen pastors like you come and go with monotonous regularity.[1] They may like you personally but they are completely immunized against your pleas for transformation, no matter how persuasive. They have heard it all before. Nothing is going to change here, nothing is going to happen.

The thing to do is to be realistic—get out of there as fast as you can. But it is standard procedure for every beginner—no matter how promising—to serve out a sentence in one or two parishes of this classification. It is hard to endure now, but will be an item in your service record of considerable value when you are competing for the top positions. You can point with pride to your humble beginnings, much as experienced politicians brag about having been broke or hungry when young, or that they were born in a log cabin. And it is during these lonely, miserable, frustrating years that you should improve the time by laying out what we might call your Professional Progress Chart. This is simply a timetable telling you where you ought to be, profession-

---

[1] Which explains the seemingly incongruous fact that the smallest churches are aware of the latest theological fads in the seminaries long before the larger churches hear of them. The small churches have heard all about Barth, Bultmann, Niebuhr and Tillich from their frequently changed young theologs, while longer-tenured pastors are relentlessly boring their larger flocks with a steady diet of Walter Rauschenbausch and Henry Nelson Wieman.

ally, at each stage of life. To guide you we include a sample chart of a normal and satisfactory clerical career for the man who is going to make it all the way.

The first three stages shown on the chart involve little more than putting in the required number of years, much as promotion in the Army is tied to seniority and nothing else—up to a point.

For the clergyman the continental divide is arrived at when he has been around the county-seat parish or Grade B city church long enough and is ready to move on and up. This should occur, as the chart indicates, between his thirty-fifth and thirty-eighth year. He needs to be called up to the major leagues now, or the summons may never come. Except for the late-blooming pastor, a rare type, who breaks into the big time after his hair thins and his paunch thickens, the fellow who hasn't been chosen for a position of some prominence before he is forty isn't going to be and might as well resign himself to spending his declining years serving a series of increasingly tedious and obscure congregations.

But what you don't realize now as you wait it out in your first parish, which is a class of job always in abundant supply and for which there are never enough ordained candidates, is that the situation reverses itself when you are ready for a desirable spot. (You should always remember that it is bad form for a minister to speak of "a better job" or "a bigger church." When you are anxious for a promotion say that you want "a larger field of service.")

Now there is an abundance of available and more-or-less presentable candidates for a rapidly shrinking supply of really worth-while pastorates. You are faced with the necessity of being chosen for advancement from out of a sizable pack of eligible preachers all of whom—at this stage of the game—appear to the naked eye to be pretty much alike. An added burden you will have to bear throughout this already difficult undertaking is that you must never betray the slightest desire for larger, better-paying and more impor-

PROFESSIONAL PROGRESS CHART

Age 26	Age 28	Age 30 or 31	Age 35–38	Age 43–50	Age 50–55
First miserable pastorate	Second miserable pastorate	County-seat parish or Grade B city church	First major league pastorate or new suburban church with tremendous potential for growth	Second major league pastorate or important board job or presidency of church-related college	Become bishop

tant responsibilities. Worldly ambition is unbecoming to the Lord's servant, and a preacher who cannot conceal his eagerness to get ahead is unfit for the plush posts he so passionately desires and is likely to be struck from the list of contenders long before the finals by those who control who gets what.

Ninety-nine out of a hundred ordinary, well-trained and generally acceptable clergymen will plug away at their jobs until one day, after four or five years in a county seat parish, notice within themselves a feeling of restlessness and a haunting, anxious question, "Will I ever get beyond this mediocre level?" Then, in a mood of quiet desperation, they look about frantically for some larger and more attractive pulpit which may be falling vacant in the near future, and go after it with all the single-minded abandon with which the greyhound chases the mechanical rabbit at the dog track. And, like the mechanical rabbit, the tasty morsel of a parish they are pursuing always eludes them. Some fellow pastor whom they had never thought of as a competitor for the job is announced as the next incumbent of the vacant major league pulpit.

After a couple such experiences a man usually resigns himself to a perpetual sheol of bitterness and oblivion, taking out his frustration by complaining constantly that "You have to be a politician to get anywhere in the church." He is right, of course. But he should have been bright enough to have figured this out in time for the knowledge to have done him some good. When a man grasps this principle only after he has suffered because of it, it is too late for him to benefit by it.

The chaps who get the job

Let us look now at the chap who did get the job. What has he been doing in these years which the defeated candidate wasted working at his job and hoping for lightning to strike him?

He has been making contacts, that's what. He took the

trouble to analyze the power structure in his conference or diocese or synod. He discovered that it was composed of officials such as a bishop and district superintendents and synodical executive secretaries plus a handful of active laymen plus one or more "kingmakers," usually clergymen who are ecclesiastical Jim Farleys, wielding influence not by virtue of their office but through their careful cultivation of significant contacts over a period of years.

He then related himself to this power structure. He had the good sense to be unobtrusive about it, at first meekly asking for a bit of advice from these princes of the church, or performing small but welcome services for them. He displayed at all times a demeanor which was respectful, alert, eager to learn, and anxious to serve. In short, he saw to it that the power structure was aware that he existed, that it knew his name, and that it was pleasant to have him around.

Before long the boys in the back room were speaking of him as "a comer" or "a promising young man." Then, by some unfathomable process of a mystical nature the time arrives when the power structure decides "we ought to do something for Jim." So, when the next major league vacancy occurs the word is dropped in the right places that "Jim Goodfellow is the man you are looking for." Why so many otherwise intelligent preachers seem unable to comprehend that this is how things are done is one of the continuing mysteries of our profession.

It occurs to the author that, while it is unnecessary to define the terms of our ecclesiastical nomenclature for our clerical readers, the thousands of laymen who will no doubt purchase this book that they may have a glimpse of what goes on behind the scenes in our profession may not understand what we mean by "major league pastorate." Following is a check list by which you can measure any church as to whether it rates major league status or not. A bona fide major league church will have:

1. A minimum of 1500 members in the congregation (2000 or more is better).

2. An impressive plant (new or old—it makes no difference).

3. A professional staff of at least two ordained clergy, a director of education and—for secure major league status—a full-time choirmaster. Next to a congregation of the wealthy and socially prominent the best status symbol a church can have is an impressively long list of paid staff members.

4. A five-figure salary for the head pastor, plus a generous expense allowance.[2]

5. At least two office secretaries.

6. An annual current expense budget in excess of one hundred thousand dollars.

7. The Sunday worship bulletin, church newspaper, and general mailings to the congregation printed rather than mimeographed. Multilith and other semi-printing processes will not do. It has to be done in a printing shop to count. Remember that we are describing the major leagues, and in the majors you have to travel first class.

8. No regular Sunday evening service, on the grounds that this practice is a hangover from an earlier generation, and that sophisticated people have something better to do with their time on Sunday evening than spend it in church. Seasonal vespers, concerts, and other special programs such as dramatics or lectures are, however, quite respectable and permissible in even the flossiest of parishes.

[2.] There is no need, however, to overcompensate the lesser members of the ministerial staff. As a matter of fact, a large church in a metropolitan center is in the fortunate position of being able to choose from any number of preachers who are willing to join its staff at the prevailing wage rates (always modest) or even less to gain the status of being associated with a prestigious congregation or to escape the ennui attendant upon serving a sleepy village parish, or both.

9. Robed choirs and gowned clergy.[3]

We close this chapter with a word of reassurance to our young clergyman determined to be a bishop. As you wait out the inescapable dreary years of your early career, as you labor unceasingly to perfect yourself in the techniques of your profession, as you sedulously cultivate the power structure which controls preferment in your synod or conference or diocese, you may become weary with well-doing, exhausted by good works and question your choice of vocation.

But when you have at last bagged a major league pastorate the pride and joy and prestige and affluence and a host of other spiritual benefits too numerous to mention which accompany the prize will bathe you in a benevolent glow and all your previous anxieties and sufferings and boredom and frustration and poverty for the sake of your calling will recede into the far reaches of your memory and seem as nothing. And you will now know what St. Paul was talking about when he wrote to Timothy:

"Now you have observed my teaching, my conduct, my aim in life, my faith, my patience, my love, my steadfastness, my persecutions, my sufferings, what befell me at Antioch, at Iconium, and at Lystra,[4] what persecutions I endured; yet from them all the Lord rescued me."

[3.] Below the Mason-Dixon line the "gowned clergy" measurement does not apply. Five thousand member churches down there will appreciate a caparisoned choir, but southerners still cherish the image of a non-clerical clergy, so the preacher usually wanders into the sanctuary in a sack suit.

[4.] Some of the Apostle's early pastorates.

ALTERNATIVE ROUTES TO THE TOP

VIII

While the author chose to travel the road of the major
league pastorate some of our distinguished leaders have preferred to climb by the routes of executive positions on one
of the boards or agencies of which every denomination
maintains an abundant supply. Or, for a deluxe trip to the
top, others select the avenue of the college presidency.
These are legitimate options for the man who plans, eventually, to wear the episcopal miter (this, of course, being a
figure of speech as no bishop of a standard-brand church
would be caught dead wearing a miter).

Convinced that the aspiring ordinand (for bishop, that
is) deserves a presentation of the possibilities via these
routes, the author—without first-hand experience—will rely
on his years of observation plus painstaking research into
the subject to offer sound guidance here.

To begin with, the ambitious clergyman who finds himself entertaining the idea of trying the board or agency
route to the top must submit to a thorough and honest self-
examination. Not everyone is temperamentally and physi-
cally suited to this type of service. For the most part it involves endless meetings of committees whose sessions are

just short of interminable, frequent staff briefings, lengthy
report meetings (usually in inverse ratio to the importance
of what is reported), inter-board liaison conferences,[1] attending church assemblies, conclaves, etc., most of which
are held in outlandish and difficult to reach locations.

The honest self-examination prior to seeking board service

So before you commit yourself to the board service route be
very certain in your own mind that you are equipped for it.
You will need to possess the capacity to endure infinite
boredom, along with what is known in horsey circles as "a
good seat" (which takes practice), sturdy kidneys and a
digestive system which can cope equally well with the
monotonous diet of the served luncheon or banquet (no
choice of what you will eat) and the uncertainties of the
fare in third-rate hotels (board executives stay in first-rate
hotels when available, but they aren't always available).

The blessings of a board executive

When making your decision as to the trail you will travel
you should weigh against the rigors of board or agency service its manifest advantages, some of which are:

(1) Freedom from the pressures, responsibilities, and
nagging worries which are an inevitable accompaniment to
the pastoral ministry. Board secretaries do not have to raise
money—they spend the money which is raised in local
churches for the purpose of supporting denominational
boards and agencies. Nor does an executive secretary have
to cultivate and please an entire congregation. He has only

[1.] Each denomination now has so many boards and agencies that
liaison conferences are essential in order that (1) duplication of programs is avoided; (2) each board can keep an eye on every other
board to see that no one group tries to outdo the others; (3) personnel
can keep informed as to attractive staff positions on other boards
which are likely to open up, thus enabling the empire builders to (a)
get the job for a friend or (b) if it is sufficiently attractive, get it for
themselves.

to please his immediate superior, (not an overwhelmingly difficult chore for a bright chap), and when he works his way up to a really choice spot he doesn't have to please much of anybody. This freedom greatly reduces the wear and tear on the central nervous system, slows down the aging process and in general has a salubrious influence on one's outlook on life. Best of all, a board secretary does not live under the necessity of grinding out a new sermon every week. He makes many speeches, to be sure, but they are always to audiences which are hearing him for the first time because with rare exceptions, board secretaries are not invited back to speak where they have once spoken. Thus, one address, with perhaps a few interchangeable funny stories to fit particular areas and situations, is serviceable for years and years. Take care, though, to have the address retyped from time to time. A yellow, crackling manuscript is a dead giveaway and is the mark of an intellectually lazy man. But this is no problem, for you will be provided with secretaries who can do this for you.

(2) A board executive, has an unparalleled opportunity for making contacts, which, if carefully cultivated, can be translated into the votes he will need when he runs for the office of bishop.

In the first place, since he travels extensively, the board man can ingratiate himself with many leaders of the denomination, a privilege denied the clergyman tethered to his parish who has little access to any but the big shots in his immediate area. Also, board executives use a fair amount of their time in preparing and mailing promotional material to thousands of pastors. This material is supposed to promote the work and interests of their particular agency, but it is accepted practice for executives to avail themselves of the opportunity to promote themselves. A ceaseless stream of letters, brochures (in four colors, preferably), and other forms of printed material, always with the executive's name at the top and his signature as apparent as Martin Luther

King at a Ku Klux Klan rally at the bottom is bound to have
a cumulative impact—even though this form of communi-
cation receives at best a casual perusal before it is discarded
by its recipients.

(3) There is no way to tell whether a board executive is
a rousing success or an abject failure. The work of a pastor
can be gauged and assessed by the application of established criteria. How much money did he raise last year?
How many new members did his church receive? Did he
add to the church plant, or pay off a mortgage? Is his Sunday School growing? Things like that. But nobody knows
for certain what a board executive is supposed to be doing,
let alone what he has actually done. And few of his professional peers, preoccupied as they are with their own concerns, care very much. They suppose "the chaps at the
Vatican"[2] are doing a bang-up job because the chaps at the
Vatican have gone to no little trouble and expense (not their
own) to convince as many of their brethren as it is possible
to reach by the United States mails that they are doing a
bang-up job.

We arrive, then, at the one and only valid objective test
of a denominational executive's effectiveness—which is the
effectiveness of his personal public relations program.

It can be safely assumed that any board secretary who
fails to exploit the opportunities for personal publicity
afforded him by his office is likely to be hopelessly incom-
petent at anything else he is doing and should not be included in that select list from which bishops are chosen.

(4) The denominational executive has an expense account. He has mileage allowance, a per diem, or provision
for hotel and restaurant expenses, and other supplements to
his income. This makes it possible for him to schedule
vacation trips which coincide with reimbursable travels in
the interests of his work, reduces substantially his grocery

2. Every protestant denomination refers to its headquarters city as
"The Vatican."

bills and enables him to enjoy life in ways not open to the pastor of a congregation.

(5) There are many men who desire to serve the Lord as one of His ordained servants, but who—because they do not like people very well, or because they are not inclined to expose themselves to the pressures of parish life, or because they are taken in by the illusion that the really important work of the church is done at the board and agency level, or for any other of a number of good and understandable reasons—prefer to serve in a "connectional" capacity (this means they are connected to *the* church but not to *a* church).

How to pretend you prefer the pastorate

You may be among this number. If you are, and if you are so fortunate as to land such a job, you must never forget that good ecclesiastical taste requires you to claim that you didn't really want it. Never, even in an unguarded moment, hint that this task suits you to a T. Board executives are expected to protest constantly as a matter of form that they long for the quiet joys of parish life, and to pretend that they plan soon to return to it. If some thoughtless and insensitive type asks, "Why, then, do you not do so?" the proper reply is that large and vital enterprises of your board are at the moment, have been for some time, and will be into the foreseeable future in crucial stages of development which require the delicate guidance of a man with experience, administrative skill and competence in this particular area—a combination of qualities which, by coincidence, no one but you possesses. Only a soldier with no sense of duty whatever would desert now in the midst of the battle when to do so would, in all probability, issue in a crushing defeat for the forces of righteousness. It is the weak and the unworthy who put their personal preferences above their clear and manifest duty, you imply.

There may be times when you will entertain the uneasy conviction that your job—or for that matter, your entire board or agency—could disappear without serious inconvenience to the Army of the Lord. Now and then you will be petrified at the possibility, however remote, that you might lose your job and be forced to earn your living as a parish pastor. But even in the face of such debilitating thoughts, don't forget to complain stoutly and with frequency of the "higher call" which an incorruptible sense of duty has prompted you to answer but which, to your eternal regret, has robbed you of the opportunity to serve a church.

The college presidency—its joys and hazards

An even surer alternative route to the top of our blessed profession is the road which leads to the president's office in a denominational college. Presidents of church-related colleges have always been considered prime bishop material.

You should be warned, though, that this appealing alternative to sweating it out in the parish ministry is not an easy sea to navigate. The American landscape is cluttered with church colleges, but the trustees sometimes heartlessly choose a professional educator for president, though a stableful of deserving preachers is available.

However, one can still be had if, for you, the right combination of circumstances obtain. These are:

(1) A presidential vacancy in a college whose board of trustees includes a wealthy layman from your congregation who has contributed vast sums of money to the college (and who, of course, is enthusiastic about you).

(2) A presidential vacancy in a college whose board of trustees includes an influential clergyman who can more-or-less name the president, and who does not fancy himself as a college president but would like to have your job.

It is apparent, then, that if you land a presidency, luck will play a large role in the accomplishment. But let us assume that providence smiles on you and you do bring it off. Your difficulties are not at an end, for you must put in a decent number of years on the job before entering the final lap of the race for the episcopacy. And you must manage these years so as to convince the churchman that you are stressing the spiritual function of the college and at the same time convince the educators that you are progressively subordinating the role of the church and are concentrating on improving the school's educational rating. You must do these things while spending about sixteen hours of your eighteen-hour working day raising money. It is an exhausting service, and you will be glad to trade the president's office for the more restful precincts of a bishop's study when the time comes.

Before you begin to move your personal effects into the president's office you should familiarize yourself with the nature of a denominational college. Otherwise, you will, in all likelihood, end up in one of the numerous bear traps or disguised pitfalls with which your path ahead is studded. Your campus may appear serene and peaceful in the twilight of a fine spring evening, but nothing could be more deceptive. It is, in fact, a raging battlefield, and that lovely lawn which grows so green in the quadrangle is fertilized by the blood of many a former president, to which may be added yours if you are not careful.

Service as president of a church college deserves a volume all its own, and one wonders why such a dissertation has not been written. Since some simple policies and administrative procedures, envisioned in advance of your incumbency, will be indispensable if you are to survive the academic climate long enough to post an impressive record, the author—who has spent more than two decades observing at close hand the operation of denominational colleges (including several years' service as trustee of one of them)— outlines here a sketchy but adequate description of the hazards you will face and helpful suggestions for overcoming them.

These hazards can be subsumed under four divisions which are here listed in order of descending importance (and danger). They are (1) the faculty, (2) the board of trustees, (3) the college's constituency (preachers and laymen, local businessmen, etc.) and (4) the students.

Living with the faculty

Fix firmly in your mind that the faculty actually runs the college. Quite naturally, it runs it to suit the tastes and convenience of the faculty.

For public relations purposes you will need to talk constantly about "a faculty of stalwart churchmen," but you will soon discover that this is a fiction of the pious imagination. The time is long gone when you could staff a college faculty with stalwart churchmen.

The department of religion is about the only one for which you can be certain of enough Christians and churchmen to meet your needs, and even here your choice may lie between some hopeless birdbrain or an intelligent but regrettably radical type who will give the school a bad name among the very people you are trying so hard to convince that you run a safe, conservative, seminary-type operation. (Since the main function of the religion department is not education but public relations, better hire the birdbrain. He will do less actual harm.)

For the departments of language, natural sciences and history you can pick up an occasional Christian layman, because these are ancient and established disciplines and their practitioners feel no particular need to prove that they are intellectually respectable by hostility to something as unacademic as the church.

It is, however, next to impossible to find a psychologist or a sociologist who is not vocal in his scorn of organized religion. This is because psychology and sociology have not yet gained the status of bona fide sciences and their disciples thus lack the academic security of, say, a chemist or a historian. And insecure academics always reassure themselves by shouting constantly that they are more academic than anybody. A popular and convenient way to do this in a denominational college is to sneer at the church.

But cultivate the faculty no matter how much it irritates you. Tell it that you work for the faculty (which is the truth) and that its welfare is your prime concern. Refer frequently to your unalterable devotion to the cause of academic freedom, for "academic freedom" is the faculty's favorite phrase. It means to the professors their right to do as they damn please, and your espousal of the cause assures them that you will not meddle with their scandalously light teaching loads, petty side rackets, personal prerogatives and the like. Above all, soft-pedal your references to the church-related nature of the college when speaking to the faculty. They consider the college's church-relatedness academically disreputable and a mark of intellectual shame and so do not like to be reminded of it. Save such speeches for money-raising junkets to the churches and business groups where it will be appreciated.

The board of trustees will be, for you, a source of continuing pleasure throughout your tenure. You will have no trouble whatever with it.

For one thing, it will be made up mostly of the same kind of people who made up the official board or session or vestry of your church, so you will feel at home with it. The bulk of the college board will be successful, affluent businessmen who look on the college as a business venture. Since they have problems in their businesses they will be sympathetic and understanding about your problems. Since their employees are frequently fractious, unreasonable and troublesome they will comprehend your problems and comfort and console you when your employees, that is the faculty, are fractious and unreasonable and troublesome.

Trustees love to build new buildings since new buildings are visible, tangible signs of prosperity, growth, success and a going institution, which coincides with your need to demonstrate that you can run a prosperous, growing, successful institution.

Also, college trustees as a rule are not given to excessive piety, and this will be a blessed relief for you and will help restore your cheerful outlook on life after your frequent and necessary association with the clergy and leading laymen of your denomination. You will come to regard your trustees with an ever deepening affection.

As for your constituency, all you need to remember is that the bulk of it and the really influential people in it will be clergymen and active laymen of your denomination. Most of them think a church college ought to be a Sunday School with dormitories, and there is no reason for you to confuse these good and loyal churchmen by any evidence that such is not entirely the case. If they do spot holes in the image console them with the information that you are making their idea of what their college should be the great guiding principle of your administration, and that it can be achieved in short order if only the churches and the alumnae will sharply increase their financial support of the institution.

Never mind the students

You need pay little attention to the students since they are a neglible factor in all but the best of schools. The faculty looks on students as necessary annoyances who only interrupt the real business of higher education which is private research, attendance at learned societies, the carrying on of faculty feuds and the like. The trustees think of them as customers. The dean of students thinks of them as behavior problems. You should think of them as opportunties for public relations. Have your picture taken crowning the home-coming queen, entertaining students at tea in the president's manse, counseling an eager freshman in your office, speaking earnestly to the student body at a chapel service (be sure the bridge games going on in the congregation are not visible in the photo), and in other situations which portray you as a benevolent and beloved father figure to these clear-eyed young Christians. Anything more than this is neither necessary nor desirable.

A few practical procedures to keep in mind when beset by problems, dilemmas, and the stresses and strains arising out of the cussedness of human nature are in order. Don't worry too much about faculty dissensions. College professors engage in feuding and fussing much as other people engage in tennis or girl watching. It is what they like to do. There is no recorded case in all educational history of a college faculty agreeing on anything. It will split ranks and contend violently over a major curriculum change or the hour established for faculty meeting with equal abandon. All experienced college administrators tell the faculty it is the decision-making body of the institution and then go ahead and do what needs to be done while the argument rages on. Usually the faculty will not even notice that a decision has been made.

Finally, keep as clear as possible from all matters of internal administration, for it is here that the fair linen of many an otherwise promising candidate has been smirched and soiled. Let the dean handle this end of the enterprise. Then if things get really rough and something simply has to be done, you can always fire the dean. Deans do not have friends and, like managers of professional baseball clubs, know when they are hired that when the good of the team requires a sacrifice, they will be it. Remember that you aren't going to be here forever. You should be safely perched on a bishop's throne by the time you have run through three or four deans.

The average term of office for college presidents is just over four years, and when you have been one, even for a considerably shorter time than this, you will understand why. Strong men decline and sturdy souls shrivel in this branch of the Lord's service. But you must persevere and give the impression that you thrive on it, else you will not be one of the front runners when the pack pursuing the episcopacy heads into the last lap of the glorious race— which is the subject to which we now turn our attention.

THE LAST LAP

IX

When you have arrived at your second major league pastorate, or important board or agency post, or college presidency you have entered the last lap of the race. By now the field of contestants for the crown has been drastically reduced. Some of the original competitors possessed talent but lacked endurance, so they dropped out. Others had the endurance but no speed and have now been lapped by the front runners. You can be certain that anyone who is still in contention at the 1/16 pole has something going for him—ability, dogged persistence, the inside track, something. From here on it is no breeze.

St. Paul, who evidently was something of a sports fan, wrote to the Corinthians a few words which you might take as your text, inspiration and guide for your final effort. "Do you not know," he wrote, "that in a race all the runners compete, but only one receives the prize? So run that you may obtain it." Then he adds, "Every athlete exercises self-control in all things."

This counsel on self-control is what you must keep in mind as you head for the finish line. By the time of your second major league pastorate (or its alternatives) you will have risen far above most of your contemporaries in the profession and will be widely recognized as an outstandingly successful man. You have to be a marked success to be considered bishop material, of course. But, acknowledged geniuses exempted, practically nobody but you is thrilled by your superior achievements. So whoever expects the blue ribbon has to corner a substantial amount of recognition and build a shiny reputation and at the same time avoid offending his clerical brethren who haven't.

This is where St. Paul's advice on self-control comes in to save you. Not very many successful men can conceal their conviction that they are where they are because they are more gifted, energetic or deserving than those whom they have outdistanced. But even if all this is obvious and undeniable, it is necessary for you to pretend that it isn't. This pretense requires unusual and unnatural self-control, which is no doubt why the apostle listed it as characteristic of the winning runner. Remember that your clerical competitors for the rich spiritual prizes the church offers to those who breast the tape ahead of the pack cannot bear the thought that you beat them because you are better at the game. It has a ruinous effect on a man's self-image. He can't stand it.

However, if he can attribute your success not to superior ability, or harder work, or a more powerful personality but simply to chance, luck or the irrational preferment of fate and higher authority, he can convince himself that, but for a less fortunate combination of circumstances beyond his control, he would be where you are, and his ego suffers no irreparable damage. He will not hate you for succeeding where he has failed—or at least he will not hate you with the virulence of the chap who is clearly bested by a man of markedly superior ability.

What you must aim for, then, is a convincing pose which projects the image of competence, success, mastery of your profession, etc., but which is diluted by a magnum or two of modesty. The church fathers, even those notably short

on it themselves, have always been strong for the virtue of
humility. Since it is widely recognized that mediocrities
and failures have no need of humility, it is a grace reserved
for winners. The fact that you possess it is a public procla-
mation that you have outdistanced the herd which began
the race. So when you pour on the coal for the last lap, begin by cultivating this cardinal Christian virtue.

Achieving the Humility-Ability Balance

So that you will not stumble in the home stretch the author
has formulated an easily remembered equation which we
shall call the Humility-Ability Balance. Put in mathemati-
cal form it would read $A \, \xi \, H = W$. A, of course, stands for
ability. ξ is a rare symbol for "modified by." H is for humility. W stands for winners. If you will commit it to memory you will not fail to balance any observable mark of
ability, success, superiority or extraordinary competence
with enough humility to take the curse off it, spare the sensibilities of your less fortunate and less gifted peers, and
clinch your image as an unusually successful practitioner of
the ecclesiastical arts and at the same time an enormously
modest man.

Perhaps an illustration or two of the Humility-Ability
Balance in operation will be helpful. Let us suppose you are
attending a conference with a group of preachers. As you
hobnob in the lobby or congregate in the coffee shop
whence you have fled the boring official sessions, one of
your peers might say to you, "I hear you are packing them
in every Sunday." The correct Humility-Ability Balance
response is "Well, church attendance is good in most places
these days."

You have managed, by this answer, to confirm the rumor
that you are doing very well without actually saying so and
without claiming any credit for this success you are said to
be enjoying. Had you boasted about your success your
peers would have catalogued you as a braggart and would

have invented reasons to explain away the good things happening in your parish.

Played the Humility-Ability Balance way, the brothers of the cloth, most of whom are struggling to keep their church attendance from sagging to alarming new lows, will not be offended, and will report to the grapevine communications system that you are not only a very able man but a "heck of a nice guy" as well. Practiced over a number of years this kind of thing builds a solid image of you as a humble hot-shot, which is exactly the impression you need to convey to those who will eventually have a hand in boosting you upward to the seats of the mighty.

The Humility-Ability Balance response comes in handy, too, when the reports of your successes are greatly exaggerated—as they often will be. By neither confirming nor denying the reports in so many words you actually confirm them without the necessity for an outright lie. And in the matter of image-building it makes no difference whatever whether the reports are accurate or ballooned out of all relationship to the facts. What does count is that your peers believe them to be true. And if you are humble about the alleged brilliance of your record the boys won't mind believing it.

The importance of the Humility-Ability Balance to any preacher desirous of the purple cannot be overstressed. Further research may reveal that it is *the* ingredient in the candidate's personality which assures his election. So in order to rivet your attention to it the author offers the following little literary effort along with the recommendation that you commit it to memory.

> There was a young preacher named Pace
> Who commenced the episcopal race.
> Through some small ability
> And lots of humility
> He captured the miter and mace.

Your author has now divested himself of all the counsel and accumulated wisdom necessary to guide and direct you as you pursue the prize of our high calling. There remains, to be sure, the problem of putting together an organization with which to confront the diocese or conference or assembly with your candidacy. But this is a highly technical matter varying from denomination to denomination and requiring an analysis so detailed and exhaustive as to constitute ample subject material for a subsequent volume or volumes (and which the author plans to offer if anticipated demand develop).

The unpredictable nature of electing assemblies

It is only fair to warn you that while strict attention to the course outlined in these pages and meticulous care in executing the plan of attack step by step should bring you eventually to a bishop's throne or an equivalent lofty office in non-episcopal denominations, it might not. The reason that it might not is that the solemn assemblies which select the winners in the race for high ecclesiastical position are, like all fallible human organizations, somewhat unpredictable and occasionally capricious in their choices. In a world where fairness and commonsense prevail a man can reasonably expect that diligent planning and half a professional lifetime spent in unrelenting devotion to the cause of getting himself named to an office of supreme spiritual power will almost automatically insure his elevation. It violates the American dream and confounds the log-cabin-to-White House mythology to believe otherwise. What happens to our democratic ideals if accidental qualities such as superior ability, outstanding intellectual equipment or bona fide spirituality tilt the balances when weighed against the diligent efforts of the man of unexceptional endowments but tireless zeal who sweats, struggles, sacrifices and strives to make himself over into a model of what the vast, pious churchgoing public insists it wants in its clergy? But, in an act of betrayal comparable to the perfidy of Benedict Arnold, these electing assemblies will frequently ignore the just claims of a good, pious servant of the Lord like you who has overcome the handicaps of small beginnings, average talents and undistinguished intellectual and spiritual attainments by fashioning yourself into just the kind of clerical personality you have every reason to think that the church prefers, and be stampeded into selecting men who have made no such effort as you have made and who commend themselves only for their brilliance, natural leadership ability, scholarship, personal winsomeness, strength of character, prophetic voice and/or other gifts, traits and qualities which, like gold, forever escape the simulation of the alchemist or witch doctor.

Concluding counsel

This is a dreary thought on which to conclude our treatise, but do not be dismayed. The odds are still very much in your favor, what with 14-karat prophets in a perpetual short supply, and with the high probability that your painful efforts to make of yourself a reasonable facsimile will issue in your being mistaken for the real thing.

At all events the goal is worth the effort, the rewards of a successful campaign are very great, and the prospect of serving the Lord in the greenest of all possible pastures should give every ambitious and reasonably robust divine a holy hot-foot as he pursues it.

And do not be deterred by nagging twinges of guilt that you, after all, are one and the same with the organization man clambering frantically up the corporate embankment, or the politician seeking secular office among smoke-suffocated and booze-benumbed delegates. When assaulted by such spiritually ennervating thoughts, as you inevitably will be, remember that you are a servant of the church, and recall that the Apostle himself said (when writing to another ambitious young preacher), "This is a true saying, if a man desire the office of a bishop, he desireth a good work."

BENEDICTION

The late Halford Luccock, borrowing from Robert Frost, claimed that he carried on a lifelong "lover's quarrel with the church."

This it seems to me, is what every Christian—be he minister or laymen—ought to do. The Christian church today is (and I suppose always has been) both glorious and ridiculous; dedicated and superficial; relevant and trivial. It behooves us then—those of us who love the church—to do what we can to eliminate the ridiculous, the superficial and the trivial so that the glory and the dedication and the relevance may be seen unobscured.

Some sincere Christians insist that this end is best accomplished by pretending that there is nothing ridiculous, superficial or trivial about the church. But so to pretend is to underestimate the perceptive powers of those outside the church, especially the well-educated materialists and the keen-minded unregenerate. That they are quicker to detect the ridiculous in the church than they are to see its glory is due in part to their lack of objectivity. But it doesn't help much for the church to play like it is perfect. These things will not go away for all our pretending.

It is healthier, I think, to acknowledge our shortcomings and poke fun at them than to claim sanctimoniously that they do not exist, or at least ought not to be admitted lest we expose ourselves to the jeers of the ungodly. More devils can be routed by a little laughter than by a carload of humorless piety.

I love the church, and the Methodist Church in particular. Not that it is any better (or any worse) than other sects, but because my life has been inseparable from it. Both my grandfathers were licensed Methodist preachers. My father, the late Phillips Brooks Smith—a man of rare wit and a good-natured sense of what was ridiculous in organized religion—was a prominent Methodist pastor in Indiana, as is my only brother, Phillips Brooks Smith, Jr. (who is so very much like his father) today.

And I am also an ordained Methodist clergyman, so the Methodist church has been my family background, and has provided me an opportunity to march in the procession of the saints[1] as well as a profession and a living. It has been a good and exciting life so far, and I expect that it will continue to be so.

An author becomes an author from a mixture of motives —the fun of creating something, the satisfaction of getting published, the desire to supplement his income, the boost to his ego from whatever public recognition or notoriety he is able to capture among others.

Also, most authors have, I imagine, somewhere on their list of motives the need to say something, to get something off their chest.

For me this something is a desire to persuade the public in general and the members of the churches in particular to

[1.] In the New Testament a saint was not a person of superior virtue simpering with self-conscious piety (which is what we often take it to mean), but an ordinary fallible human being subject to and often afflicted with all the ills the mortal spirit is heir to, who was a member of the Christian Church and was trying to follow Jesus Christ as best he knew how.

accept the clergy as part of the human race—a recognition they have persistently refused to accord us. As one bright and attractive young lady (a high school senior) who is a member of my present congregation said to me recently, "It is hard for me to think of ministers as people." So it is, my dear, but I wish it weren't.

I now know why authors always include words of appreciation to many people who, they claim, helped them bring the book into being. Until now I thought this was only polite hogwash. But it is really true.

If my wife, my son and daughter, my mother, and several close friends had not provided for me an enthusiastic captive audience in the first days of the writing and encouraged me to go on, I probably would have quit early.

The Rev. Carl Quinluin Baker, long time friend and coworker, thinks he rates a co-authorship for his many suggestions, his constant encouragement and his willingness to assume not a few of my regular responsibilities so as to enable me to complete the manuscript before the deadline. And he is right.

Dr. Gerald L. Clapsaddle, a general secretary of the Methodist Board of Missions and friend of the years, had much valuable information to impart about the workings of boards and agencies of the church. The best way for me to thank him is to state with emphasis that nothing in the chapters on boards and agencies applies to him in any way whatever.

Dr. John Sylvester Smith, also a friend of many years' standing, who is a veteran college administrator as well as a Methodist clergyman, helped me to understand the complexities of a denominational college.

And Mrs. Sam Danenberger, valued member of my congregation, rapidly and expertly typed the manuscript and had the grace to chuckle as she typed. There is no substitute for a competent typist, especially for one who laughs at what you hope is funny.

If any reader feels that the astringency with which some

subjects have been treated is excessive I can only say that
I think they deserve the treatment. If there are those who
protest the needle which has been occasionally jabbed into
the body of the church, I protest that it was aimed at those
areas which need to be sensitized.

No matter what comes of it, it has been a lot of fun doing this book. And, as any good umpire will insist, I only
call it as I see it.

> Charles Merrill Smith
> Wesley Methodist Church
> Bloomington, Illinois
>
> *May 20, 1964*

DATE DUE

MAY 14 '65		
FEB 2 5 '66		
MAR 2 5 '66		
MAY 6 '66		
FEB 17 1972		
JAN 2 4		
GAYLORD		PRINTED IN U.S.A.